To our friend Bill,
Happy Birthday
2-2011

Betty & Don

TOUCHED BY GRACE

TOUCHED BY GRACE
THE STORY OF HOUSTON ATTORNEY JOE H. REYNOLDS

JOE HUNTER REYNOLDS

Outskirts Press, Inc.
Denver, Colorado

The opinions expressed in this manuscript are solely the opinions of the author and do not represent the opinions or thoughts of the publisher. The author has represented and warranted full ownership and/or legal right to publish all the materials in this book.

Touched By Grace
The Story of Houston Attorney Joe H. Reynolds
All Rights Reserved.
Copyright © 2010 Joe Hunter Reynolds
v3.0

This book may not be reproduced, transmitted, or stored in whole or in part by any means, including graphic, electronic, or mechanical without the express written consent of the publisher except in the case of brief quotations embodied in critical articles and reviews.

Outskirts Press, Inc.
http://www.outskirtspress.com

ISBN PB: 978-1-4327-6371-8
ISBN Hb: 978-1-4327-6372-5

Outskirts Press and the "OP" logo are trademarks belonging to Outskirts Press, Inc.

PRINTED IN THE UNITED STATES OF AMERICA

Touched by Grace

The Story of
Houston Attorney
Joe H. Reynolds

*For Our Children and Our Children's Children,
and Their Children, and their children, and their children . . . .*

By
Joe Hunter Reynolds

*as told to, researched, and edited by Carol Ann Wilson
with additional assistance by Kay K. Morgan*

Contents

Foreword ix
Examples of Grace xi
Preface xiii
Chapter 1:   Days of Youth 1
Chapter 2:   School Years 15
Chapter 3:   The War Years 27
Chapter 4:   Joe, Susie, Hunt, and Dan 45
Chapter 5:   The Grandchildren 59
Chapter 6:   Joe's Law Career Starts with a Bang 65
Chapter 7:   Joe's "Adventures" in Korea 75
Chapter 8:   Back To Joe's Law Career and Houston I.S.D. ... 91
Chapter 9:   Joe's Career Shifts To High Gear 111
Chapter 10: The Tenneco Years 119
Chapter 11: Meet Mr. Hess 127
Chapter 12: 10b-5 137
Chapter 13: Joe Jamail 143
Chapter 14: Lawsuits and More Lawsuits 153
Chapter 15: Winding Down 165
Chapter 16: Legal Leftovers 177
Chapter 17: Instant Aggies 185
Chapter 18: The Baptist and His Bible 195

Chapter 19: Health Matters 211
Chapter 20: Conclusion 219
Epilogue 227
Appendix A: Mostly Complete List of Joe H. Reynolds'
                    Reported Cases (chronological) 229
Appendix B: Poems of Joe H. Reynolds 237
Appendix C: Military Timeline of Joe H. Reynolds 249

Foreword

The title to these memoirs is the story of my life.

I am a nobody, an average East Texas boy,
who has nothing special in the way of ability.

These stories are from my best memory, and they contain my opinions. I have been faithful to the Truth as I know it, and have no intention ever to hurt anyone.

But what you read and what you learn from these memoirs
is unexplainable,
except that my life has been truly Touched by Grace.

Joe H. Reynolds

Examples of Grace

Someone sent this to me by e-mail, and I said to myself that these are good examples of grace, and, although I do not know its source or whom to credit, I wanted to share it with the readers of this book.

Picture yourself blindfolded in front of a firing squad. You are guilty and you deserve to die. You await the gunshots. You hear footsteps approaching you, and your heart pounds in your chest. Then you feel the ties being loosened and the blindfold removed.

Jesus stands there. He says "You go on now. I will take care of this for you." *This is grace.*

Or perhaps you die and stand in front of St. Peter. He says you will need 100 points to get into Heaven, and he asks what you have done. You tell him you have attended church faithfully and tithed. St. Peter says, "Good, that is worth one point."

You add that you gave away all of your possessions and fed the poor. St. Peter says, "Wonderful, one point."

So you say, "I prayed every day and taught my children to pray and go to church." Again, one point.

You begin to despair, and lament, "There is no way for me to get in there except by the grace of God."

St. Peter smiles. "97 points, come on in."

This is Grace.

Preface

by Carol Ann Wilson - Secretary to Joe H. Reynolds since 1980

It's hard to write this, because Joe Reynolds and I have been working on this book for about 15 years.

This book is his dictation, his words, his sentiments, his flavor-him. I would type as he would dictate, and I would properly punctuate and make grammatical corrections as we went along. From time to time we would discuss things if I had a question from a reader's viewpoint, and he would make them more clear.

And from time to time, we would put "the book" down for a while, so he could think about it. Then he would make revisions and we would work on it for another while, until something more important came along. Since he was so generously other-directed, and he was always called upon to do things for others, it seemed that there was always something "more important." At one time the book project sat around for about five years, but thank God for the magic of *saving*. It was never lost, and we would pick it back up and work on it some more.

For the last few years of our project, 2006 to 2009, we worked very hard to finish it, as I continually nagged at him to move it to the top of his list. But sadly, as a judge would call with a request that he serve as Special Master or Receiver in a particularly complicated case, or as a lawyer friend would die without a will and he would be asked to serve as Administrator, our project was moved down on his list of things to do.

Joe Reynolds died a bit after midnight on Saturday morning, December 19, 2009. He and I had finished the book except for just a few needed tweaks I had made notes to ask him about. I had printed out the almost-final version, and he had promised to devote the coming week to "finishing the book." Wahoo! We were finally going to get it finished before I left to visit my family in Memphis for Christmas. Then we would put it in final form and scan photos and get it to a printer the first thing in 2010. But unforeseen things usually happen when matters are put off.

So with the help of Susie and Joe's former law partners Tom Cordell, Ed Junell, Grant Cook, and Kay Morgan, and with the special extra help of Wade Whilden and Judge Lamar McCorkle, we have been able to take care of those tweaks and "get it done."

After that five-year layover "the book" had, he was reading it, and he said, "You know, this is pretty good!" I told him that I thought it was great, and that many, many people wanted-and needed-to read it (especially young lawyers), and we should get it finished. His friends continually asked about it. "When are you gonna finish the book?" So we finally got back to it seriously, the last few years. I hope you enjoy reading it and getting to know this wonderfully exceptional man.

In their Houston home, Joe and I did a lot of work in his section of the house known as "Joe's office." Depositions have been taken, hearings have been held, interviews have taken place, and work has been done just as if we were back downtown in the law office. He was Of Counsel to Schwartz, Junell, Greenberg & Oathout those last years, and he loved that firm and all the lawyers in it- especially those up-and-coming Young Turks. But his volunteer work and personal work was done right out of his home office. And that chair where he so often sat is where some of us still feel his presence today.

Joe Reynolds, we miss you.

Thank you for leaving us your story.

CHAPTER 1

Days of Youth

In telling any kind of story, the temptation is to begin at the beginning. In the case of a life story, it seems natural that the beginning is birth, so that's where I'll start.

I was born Joe Hunter Reynolds on November 21, 1921, and most people believe it was in Tyler, Texas. However, since the Cotton Belt Railroad was on strike, Papa John, my father, who worked for the railroad, was on temporary assignment in Commerce, Texas, where I was actually born.

I was born at home, the fifth of six children to John Gordon Reynolds and Espie Duke Reynolds. Our neighbor on the right was a man named Dick Hunter, a barber, who owned the Hunter Barber Shop in Commerce. To our left lived a family named Fuller. Their oldest daughter was Ida Jo Fuller. My mother, who loved the Hunters and who loved the Fullers, named me Joe Hunter Reynolds. And I've lived with that name ever since. In fact, I was called Joe Hunter all the way through high school, and my good friends, Gibson Gayle, Rook Edwards, and Tuffy McCormick, still call me Joe Hunter to this very day. On my 77th birthday, Gib and Tuffy both called me and said, "Happy Birthday, Joe Hunter." On my 87th birthday Gib and Tom McDade took me to lunch and said, "Happy Birthday, Joe Hunter."

We lived in Commerce for about a year after my birth. My brother Earl had also been born in Commerce two and a half years before me. When I was one, Papa John was transferred back to Tyler, and we lived there another two years. Then we moved to Waco. I've always been told that this move broke my mother's heart, because she had been born and reared in Smith County, and she knew no one in Waco. She couldn't wait to get back to Tyler.

Mother was called "Beppie," and my dad was called "Papa John." Beppie was Espie Duke, and her father was a lawyer, whom I never knew (Allen Morgan Duke II). But from my earliest memory I've always been told that Granddaddy Duke was one of the great men of the world.

His law partner was Jim Hogg, who was later governor of Texas. During his career my grandfather ultimately went into the insurance business and helped organize a fraternal brotherhood called the Eagles, and at some point in his life he was the head honcho of a fraternal organization called Woodmen of the World. He started in Texas a type of insurance company known as a fraternal company, which was basically a group company.

More important, he was a great Christian, and he was a founding member of Marvin Methodist Church in Tyler. Martha Greenhill, my cousin, tells me I'm the spitting image of my grandfather-that I look like him, act like him, and believe like him.

My Uncle Ba (pronounced "bah"), whose real name was Allen Morgan Duke III, worked for my grandfather in the insurance business. As a young man, he moved to Fort Worth, Texas, where he organized a life insurance company called Trinity Life. He organized a second company in Dallas, the name of which I can't remember. And some time before World War II he put all these companies together and called them Southland Life, which still exists today and is headquartered in Atlanta. Uncle Ba was my "rich uncle."

My mother was the greatest woman in the world. She loved the Lord. She loved the Bible. And I can still remember her Bible stories and how she would read the Bible to us and make it come alive. Her favorite chapter was John 21. She was quite a gal.

In the summertime she would make us all sit around on the floor, and she'd tell us Bible stories. One of the stories I remember her teaching us arose from a picture we had in the hall of our house. She or one of the children would get that picture off the wall. It was a picture of Jesus standing at the door of a Hathaway cottage, and Jesus is standing at the door, knocking. My mother would always ask the question, "What is the thing you notice about the door of the house?" We would say, "we don't know." She would then tell us, "Notice there is no door handle on the outside. The door has to be opened from within."

She was my friend and I could never, ever do anything that would discredit her. Earl related to her maybe more than I did, but I was her pride and joy. I lived to please her.

My dad was a brilliant man, conservative in every bone of his body. He had opinions about everything, and I agreed with nearly all of them. He worked hard; he worked six days a week, and sometimes only five days a week. But he loved to go fishing. Until I was 15, every Friday or Saturday night (whichever night he got off for the weekend), he, my brother Bill, and I went fishing.

It was an ordeal. Fishing wasn't fun; it was work. We (Bill and I) seined minnows; we dug up worms. The three of us would bait trot lines in the Neches River and later in the Bosque River. We would run the lines at midnight, rebait them, rerun them at 5 in the morning. We had no cots; we slept on the ground on quilts. Early Sunday morning we'd gather up our gear, including the fish we had caught and cleaned, and go back home in time to wash and clean up and go to Sunday School. It was a rare Sunday, indeed, to miss Sunday School.

In Tyler we went to Marvin Methodist Church, and later in Waco we went to St. John's Church on Bosque Avenue, also a Methodist Church. In those days, the Methodist Church was an evangelical, Bible-believing, hellfire-and-damnation Church. Had it been a liberal church at that time, my daddy would have been the first to withdraw.

My dad hated, but not necessarily in this order: Lyndon Johnson, labor unions, and the University of Texas football team. Papa John was quite a guy. One of his favorite expressions was that Lyndon Johnson was a wolf in wolf's clothing. Papa John was a self-made man. He quit school in the eighth grade, got a job working for the railroad, having walked from the farm into town to get that job. He worked for the Cotton Belt Railroad until the day he retired at age 62 (born in 1886, retired in 1948).

We moved to Waco in 1924 and rented a house on 25th Street. My brother Bill was born in 1924 in Waco, and I can remember it. I was three years old. I remember waking up one Thanksgiving morning, November 25, and Papa John said we had something special. I asked if it was a turkey.

I started to public school at North Waco Elementary, where my first grade teacher was Miss Strange. I stayed in that school through the fourth grade, skipping the third grade, because they didn't think I needed it. I was double-promoted. I had no trouble in the fourth grade.

We then moved to Lasker Avenue, and I went to Dean Highland Elementary School, then to West Junior, and finally to Waco High School. In the summertime my dad would often go to Tyler and work there for the entire summer. The man who was foreman of the shops in Tyler would go on vacation and my daddy would be transferred back to Tyler to run the shops until the other man came back from vacation. This meant we spent a month or more every summer in Tyler. We would all stay with my grandparents.

Junior high and high school were easy for me. My oldest brother, Johnny, was a star football player at Waco High School, during the golden years of Waco's great football teams. His senior year in high school, he was selected as the #1 football player in Texas high school football. He was offered scholarships to many universities, but chose to go to Baylor in Waco, so that he could work at night driving a cab to give Earl, Bill, and me lunch money for school.

My brother Earl was a gifted student, and when I followed in his footsteps, all of the teachers knew me, either because of my brother Earl or my brother Johnny. So my high school days were a piece of cake.

I was selected as one of the top outstanding boys in my high school. I was president of my senior class, president of the Rostra Debating Society, and president of the Hi-Y, which was the service club in my high school. I graduated high in my class, next to Dorothy Martin, a girl who lives up the street from us now here in Houston. I could never beat her, although I tried. (She doesn't call me Joe Hunter.) In 2001, though, I was honored to be named outstanding graduate of Waco High School.

My sister Dorace ("Dada") was the oldest child in our family. She was a corker. She ruled the roost. She kept four boys in line. She was Beppie's top sergeant. She ran a nursing home in Corpus Christi, Texas, and during my later stay in the naval hospital in Corpus after I was injured at the Chosin Reservoir in Korea, she became my top sergeant. But she gave me the first car I ever owned, the Charger.

Bill was the youngest. Like Johnny, he was quite an athlete. He married a wonderful girl, and unfortunately for us, they moved away to Arkansas.

During my senior year in high school, Papa John was transferred back to Tyler permanently. Beppie knew that it would be a tragedy for me to have to go back to Tyler High School for my senior year. So she arranged for me to live with some friends of ours in Waco. I lived with David Lewis and his family on Cumberland Street for three or four months and lived three or four months with Billy Joe Webb and his family on their "farm"—which was more like a castle to me. (Interestingly, in later years following the war, Billy Joe Webb's mother was in Tyler working, and she stayed with Papa John and Beppie.)

I can't pass up my boyhood days in Waco without talking about the day I accepted the Lord. I was twelve years old. It was Youth Sunday at St. John's Methodist Church, and a young man who was about 16 was leading the music. He said, "Turn to page 269 and we'll sing the first two stanzas of *When the Roll is Called Up Yonder*." As we sang that first verse, I had the very distinct impression that the Lord was calling me to join Him and to put my life in His hands forever. And then they sang that second stanza, which goes like this:

> *On that bright and shiny morning,*
> *When the dead in Christ shall rise,*
> *And the glory of His resurrection share;*
> *When the saints on earth are gathered*
> *In their home beyond the skies,*
> *When the roll is called up yonder, I'll be there.*

I got up and walked to the front of the church and accepted the Lord as my savior, in the fashion they used to do in the Methodist church. And that was the best decision of my life, and it is the story of my life.

But now it's time for a flashback. I couldn't recite all these things without telling a little bit about Papa John's family. I remember Granddaddy Reynolds, John Calhoun Reynolds, real well. I was afraid of him.

My most vivid remembrance is the day he died. I believe it was in 1927. They lived in a house on East Erwin in Tyler, and his room was upstairs. It had a mantel and a fireplace. I remember standing there that day, with Beppie and others. On the mantel above the fireplace was a white horse made of Plaster of Paris. I loved that horse. And on that white horse was a man in a white sheet.

I asked Beppie if there was any way that I could have that white horse. She said, "No." She said I didn't need that white horse. But I still loved that horse.

That horse with the man in the white sheet was, of course, a replica of the Ku Klux Klan. Granddaddy Reynolds was a full-fledged member, but his involvement was borne strictly out of the original purpose, which was to protect the widows and orphans of Confederate soldiers during Reconstruction.

He had been a Confederate veteran. He was a very young boy when he joined the Sixth Alabama Regiment and served under General John B. Gordon—hence, my daddy's middle name. He was captured on July 3, 1863, at the Battle of Gettysburg, and spent the rest of the war in prison, first at Fort Delaware for 5 months, and then for 15 months at Point Lookout, Maryland.

◀ TOUCHED BY GRACE

When he came up for parole from that Yankee prison in 1864, there was a man in prison with him by the name of Buford Jester, who had a family back in Corsicana, Texas. My grandfather changed places with Mr. Jester so that Mr. Jester could go home to his family. And in a Bible at our home, sadly long since lost, was a letter from Mr. Jester to my grandfather, acknowledging these facts. Where that letter is today is anybody's guess. Incidentally, this man's son, also named Buford Jester, later became governor of Texas.

My brother Bill and I shared a visit at Bill's daughter Julie's home in Navasota, Texas. Bill had a letter Granddaddy Reynolds wrote his father, Thomas A. Reynolds, from prison, and that letter is a testimony to these memories. The letter was published in a newspaper-I believe it was the *Tyler Courier Times*-in 1911, and the original was in a very fragile condition, although it had been kept in plastic. Here is the letter:

"Point Lookout, Md. Oct. 1, 1864

"Dear Father,

"I received your very welcome letter of the 3rd, inst. in due time, and I certainly rejoiced-it's been the first letter I have received from you to learn that you are all living and enjoying good health.

"You express a desire to see us all at home once more. My prayer is that you may reach your wish and live many, many years with all of us together enjoying life, and that our last days may be your best days.

"There are rumors in camps here at this time of an immediate exchange of fifteen hundred prisoners. They are now taking all the sick who are able to travel, out of this camp for parole.

"I hope the parole may stand to all those so fortunate, indeed.

"I am somewhat sanguine in my expectation of its reaching me. I have been a prisoner for a long time and in the event of my being paroled, would feel myself 'like Elijah of old'-translated to bliss.

"You asked me about Berry Crow. I am sorry to have the fact to state that he died in the hospital at Gettisburg from the affects of a wound received in the battle of Gettisburg.

"I am in very good health at present and hope this may find you and Ma and sisters and Uncle Jack's folks all in good health and spirits. Do not forget to mention me to all of my old friends, particularly the young ladies.

"I have the pleasure to subscribe myself your dutiful and affectionate son.

J. C. REYNOLDS"

The newspaper article went on to say that this letter to his father by J. C. Reynolds was preserved by his mother and before her death, she gave it to her son.

The article further stated that Mr. Reynolds was then 73 years old "but looks to be about 55," and that his father, who would have been my great-granddaddy Thomas A. Reynolds, had died in 1905 at the age of 95 years at Palestine, leaving some 100 descendants.

Granddaddy Reynolds was married in 1866 to Miss Susie Saxon in Alabama, and they moved to Tyler in 1892. At the time the newspaper article was written, they had ten children, all of whom were still living.

TOUCHED BY GRACE

I guess I came by my "fighting spirit" naturally. My great-granddaddy Thomas A. Reynolds, who was brought up in South Carolina before moving to Alabama in 1840, had volunteered in 1834 to fight the Seminole Indians in that terrible struggle in the Florida Everglades. At his death, he still carried the scars from those battles.

For my family, I'd like to tell one other story about that Gordon name in our family. One of our associate pastors at Second Baptist Church is Dr. Jim DeLoach. In 2001 he told me he was planning to attend a family reunion in Americus, Georgia, at the New Harmony Baptist Church.

The New Harmony Baptist Church had been the home church of Confederate General John B. Gordon, one of the great generals of the Confederacy. General Gordon had been baptized in that church as a small boy. He was so small, in fact, that the boy had to stand on the communion table for the congregation to see him to vote the boy into membership. Dr. DeLoach said that the last time he had been at New Harmony, that communion table still stood at the front of that little Baptist Church in Americus, Georgia.

Shortly after the Civil War was over, General John B. Gordon, a strong opponent of Reconstruction, was being considered for the United States Senate. In those days, senators were elected by state legislatures, not by popular vote. The Georgia Legislature was in session to determine whether he should be elected, and General Gordon was sitting at the podium.

One of the legislators who had served in General Gordon's regiment, the Fifth Alabama Regiment, did not like General Gordon, and he had the specific intent to speak against General Gordon's nomination-although he knew he would be a voice crying in the wilderness-because he so disliked General Gordon.

As he stood there, very close to General Gordon, he became very emotional as he noticed the scar across General Gordon's face. Then in a broken voice, this old soldier became very emotional and said that he had come to speak against General Gordon but could not, because he "had forgotten the scar." That horrible scar was on the left side of General Gordon's face. And if you search today for pictures of General John B. Gordon, you will find that they show only the right side of his face.

I tell this story to explain the importance of the Gordon name in the Reynolds family. My daddy was named John Gordon Reynolds by his father, John Calhoun Reynolds, who was in the Fifth Alabama Regiment of General John B. Gordon. My brother Bill was named Bill Gordon Reynolds for General John B. Gordon, and my nephew, Gordon Reynolds, is also named for General John B. Gordon.

In Susie's genealogical studies, we have since discovered that my great grandfather on Beppie's side, Allen Morgan Duke I, was in the Confederate Army and was captured on July 4, 1863, at Vicksburg. This great grandfather signed a waiver and agreed not to take up arms again against the Yankees, in return for being paroled. But my Granddaddy Reynolds had refused such a proffer, and told the Yankees, "this war will never end, as far as I'm concerned."

So Granddaddy Reynolds spent the rest of the war in prison, returning to Alabama at the end of the war, as did Great Grandfather Duke, where they all but starved to death, due to carpetbaggers, Sherman burning their farms, and all the other oppressive Yankee acts. As a consequence of Sherman's devastation of our family, the Duke family came to Tyler, Texas, in the 1870s . The Reynolds clan, led by Thomas Arthur Reynolds, came to Texas in 1882, ending up in Palestine, Texas. Granddaddy John Calhoun Reynolds came later, sometime after 1886, to Tyler.

Now Hear This

So that anyone who reads this account may know the truth: the American Civil War, called by us the War Between the States, had little to do with slavery. No Reynolds or Duke ever owned a slave. That war was all about money. Four Southern states-Virginia, North Carolina, South Carolina, and Georgia-paid 75 percent of the total revenues collected by the federal government. The Northern states paid practically zero.

In addition, the Southern states, by an act of Congress, were required to pay the Revolutionary War debts of the Northern states as well as their own! Most Northeastern states, but especially New York and Massachusetts, never paid Revolutionary War bills. The South paid these bills through the tariff. The South sold cotton to England, and England sold furniture to the South. The North wanted that, and so the tariff was put into effect.

Because the Southern States exported cotton, tobacco, sugar cane, and rice to Great Britain and Europe, they were financially successful in their businesses. Customers of the Southern states were competitors of the Northeastern states, and the South naturally did business with Europe and England.

The Northeastern states manufactured and sold furniture, clothing, and other manufactured goods, as did Great Britain. However, the Southern States bought such goods from their customers across the Atlantic. The Northeastern States wanted to exclude their European competition from selling their products to the Southern states.

The root cause of the War Between the States (sometimes called the War of the Northern Aggression because the Union Army, on orders from President Lincoln, did in fact invade South Carolina), therefore, was really the issue of states' rights, guaranteed by the Tenth Amendment to the United States Constitution.

The other point I want to make can be posed as a question: At Appomattox, hanging on the wall of McLean's Tavern, are the pictures of Grant and Lee. Which of those two generals owned slaves at the conclusion of the War Between the States? Your answer can be Neither, Both, Grant, or Lee. If you answer Grant and only Grant, you are correct. Most people do not know that the Emancipation Proclamation issued by Lincoln in 1863 freed the slaves in the Southern states but did not free the slaves in the Northern states.

While some families in the Southern States were wealthy before the War Between the States, after the War, everybody was poverty-stricken. This caused a westward migration by people from Alabama and Mississippi to East Texas. No one in Susie's family or my family ever forgot that War. We were raised on that War, and to the day our parents died, they continually reminded us of our Southern heritage.

I am a proud grandson of not one but two Confederate veterans. I believe the Confederate flag to be a symbol of pride in one's country and devotion to a cause. No one should ever think that flag to be based in hate, nor should anyone hate that flag because of "political incorrectness." One thing should be thought whenever anyone sees that flag: "Lest we forget."

History cannot be changed, and the modern-day history revisionists are doing a disservice to millions of Americans by trying to do so. I have long been a proud member of the Sons of Confederate Veterans, and I am proud of all my fellow members. It is our heritage and it is nothing that should cause shame.

CHAPTER 2

School Years

My school years previously described occurred during the Great Depression, and a description of those years would not be complete without a discussion and explanation of how we lived. Papa John had a job, but times were tough.

When I was a boy, on too many days to remember, we had to take cold biscuits, cold mashed potatoes, and cold pinto beans for our lunch at school. Later, when Johnny was in Baylor and driving a cab, he gave us 15 cents a day for lunch money, and I would spend it all on ice cream. Today, I can eat Blue Bell all day long (when I can get away with it). And today, I would starve before I would eat a cold biscuit, cold mashed potatoes, or cold pinto beans. As a matter of fact, I won't eat them when they are warm, either.

Speaking of how poor the Reynolds family was, and we were, I'll never forget the night Papa John came home and told Beppie, at the dinner table with all of us present, that starting on Monday he would stay home two days a week so that his friend Johnny Quick could work in his place and feed his family. My mother told him that was going too far, and Papa John said, "Let's try it and see how we make out." And we did.

◄ TOUCHED BY GRACE

During the Depression years, *i.e.*, 1932 until 1939, Waco was devastated. It had been built by the cotton business. That's why the railroads were there. But the cotton markets in Texas totally disappeared. There were no markets for cotton, and what had once been a thriving little town became a very, very hard-hit, poor community. During those Waco years, I had a job working on Saturdays while school was in session, and all during the summer, in a grocery store.

On the other hand, Tyler prospered during those same Depression years, because in 1929 the East Texas oilfield hit. Even though oil was selling for as low as five cents a barrel, Tyler boomed, and so did the Cotton Belt. Papa John went back to Tyler in 1937. Beppie and Bill moved back to Tyler in 1938. I graduated from Waco High School in 1939, while Earl was in college at Texas U. (After World War II, he came back and finished at Texas A&M.)

In Tyler, I continued my career as a grocery sacker. I worked for Brookshire Brothers and they gave me a job every summer and every holiday I wanted to work, even while I was at Baylor. I finally graduated to being assistant butcher, and would make enough money in the summers to pay for my education at Baylor in the fall. Before Baylor, I went to Tyler Junior College and worked at Brookshire Brothers in the afternoons.

Despite the bad times, I had a great childhood. God always provided the very best for us. For example, I had a pass on the Cotton Belt Railroad, as did every other member of my family. We could travel anywhere the Cotton Belt went and also transfer to connecting railroad lines, so that travel was easy for us. For example, when we were spending the summers in Tyler, my brother Bill and I would keep up with major league baseball, and on many occasions we'd go down to the Cotton Belt depot at 10 in the morning, carrying a couple of peanut butter sandwiches, and get on the train, sit up all night, and arrive at Union Station in St. Louis the following morning. From there we would hike a mile or so to Sportsmen's Park to see major league baseball.

My favorite team was the New York Giants. Bill's favorite team was the St. Louis Cardinals. And we would pick our game, go to St. Louis, arrive at the ball park before it opened, and then sit in the bleachers for 25 cents, watch the game, walk back to the depot, and leave back for Tyler around 6 in the evening, arriving home the next day in the afternoon. It was great! We had a ball. All of the conductors knew us. They would give us pillows to make the trip easier, as we slept in our seats. And we would talk to conductors about baseball.

We were about 13, 14, or 15 at the time, and we knew every player, their batting averages, their pitching statistics. My hero was Carl Hubbell, a pitcher for the Giants. Bill liked Dizzy Dean. We saw some wonderful baseball games. Those days were different from today. My mother never had to worry about us. She knew we were perfectly safe, and that nothing bad could happen to us.

While living in Waco, we had access to the YMCA, and in my high school years at Waco High, I served as counselor at Y Camp on the Bosque River at Valley Mills, Texas, at the Falls of the Bosque. During the years I was a counselor at Y Camp, one of the boys in my cabin, perhaps every year I was a counselor, was my younger friend, Gibson Gayle. The campers came for two weeks at a time, and I was there for the entire summer. I was paid a very small salary, and my principal job was not as a football coach or even a baseball coach, although I did that, but primarily as a Bible teacher. I was a pretty good swimming teacher, too. Not many boys my age could teach the Bible. But Beppie had given me enough Bible stories to teach the campers.

Not to be overlooked: I was a great athlete (in all modesty). I participated in every sport. I played center field on the baseball team, linebacker in football, and guard on the basketball team. And I excelled at tennis. We played afternoons and summers at the tennis courts in the park, but not in any organized activity.

I remember one night we were playing doubles at Cameron Park, and there was an older couple, man and woman, playing singles on the adjoining court. Much to my surprise, the woman was a Mrs. Arrington, one of my teachers in junior high school, which I then attended. I wasn't sure she knew me, but the next day in class, she told the class that I had the best manners of any young person that she had seen for a long time, primarily because, as I was sweating during my tennis game, she observed that I used a handkerchief (which was really a rag) rather than my arm, to wipe the sweat from my brow. From that time on, I was her favorite. I quit playing tennis in 1990 after a rotator cuff problem, but I continued to carry a rag.

My brother Earl paved the way for me to do lots of things in high school. He had a great memory, and consequently he was asked to participate in all the drama productions in high school. When I came along, the teachers automatically assigned me parts in all the plays. I should have been an actor (in all modesty).

If you have known me for some time, you probably know that in 1987 I received a special acting award given to me by a Sunday School Class at Houston's Second Baptist Church then named "Nothing But the Truth" for my outstanding portrayal of Benjamin Franklin in the Second Baptist Church production of *We the People*. (I also did a good job of playing Colonel Proudfeather in *The Enchanted Forest* [in all modesty].)

I can't leave my discussion of high school without reflecting on the one-act play, *The Red Carnation*. I was either a sophomore or a junior in high school, but I was chosen to play the romantic male lead. And the girl chosen to play the female romantic lead was an identical twin. This girl's name was Lois Bailey. She was beautiful and two years my senior. I was just beginning to notice girls.

The director and teacher was Mr. Bruce Roach, and at the conclusion of the play, I was required to kiss Lois Bailey. Unfortunately, I did not know how to kiss, so he commanded Lois and me to practice! Much against my will! After *hours* of practice, I finally got it right. But I did not receive an Academy Award, and I never really learned how to kiss—until in 1947, when I returned from the Marine Corps, and a little blonde-haired Baylor beauty inspired me to learn the art of kissing.

When my high school days finally ended, I moved for good to Tyler, rejoined my family, and wondered about the future. My Uncle Harry, who always took notice of me, suggested that I get a summer job working for Brookshire Brothers in Tyler, as I stated earlier in this account. I saved my money, and after two years of junior college, and with Brother Johnny getting me a job at Baylor, I was finally able to go to Baylor, hopefully to finish my education.

Tyler Junior College was a great place. I had great teachers; none were better. I was on the debate team. I managed to do well in school, and I continued my acting, my debate activities, and extemporaneous speaking. One of my debate partners was Vernon Turner, who would play a big part in my life, and another was Frankie Abraham, later a Houston lawyer, who was a year behind me in junior college.

The most significant thing to me was that we debated against great debaters and had to speak extemporaneously. My frequent opponent was a young man by the name of John Hill from Kilgore Junior College. His partner was a young man by the name of Charles Wellborn. Both of them became eminently successful. But when we had our finals in Temple, Texas, at Temple Junior College, I had the good fortune of winning the state championship in extemporaneous speech, beating my friend John Hill for this coveted honor.

Many remarkable incidents occurred during our debating competitions. We went by private automobile. I had none, and was always a guest passenger, and on one occasion the debate team went to Beaumont to debate against Lamar Junior College. I had the fortune-or misfortune-of riding in the car with a girl debater from Tyler named Iris Jean Fudor, later Iris Sift, who was murdered while she was director of Houston's famous Alley Theater.

But on this occasion we were driving from Beaumont back to Tyler, and we got into a horrendous argument over politics! Naturally, she was the liberal and I was the conservative. Somewhere between Beaumont and Nacogdoches, she stopped the car, ordered me out, and left me on the side of the road! Fortunately for me, a car came by, picked me up, and I rode in comfort with Ann Miller, Vernon Turner's sister, all the way back to Tyler.

Another memorable experience was at Texas A&M, where I was engaged in an invitational extemporaneous speaking contest. When it was all over, I thought I had won, and the judge, a professor at Texas A&M, walked up to me and told me that I was a gifted speaker, except for one thing. He said I butchered the King's English. I made the mistake, repeatedly in that speech, of putting the wrong tense on the verb "begin."

I later came to realize it was because I knew the words to the song, *Amazing Grace*, especially this verse: "When we've been there ten thousand years, bright shining as the sun; we've no less days to sing God's praise, than when we'd first begun." The problem was, I did not realize that song had a contraction (we'd). So because I knew that song so well, I used the word-even in everyday speaking English-in the past perfect tense (begun), when it should have been the past tense (began). I wanted to argue with this professor, but then something told me he knew more than I did. (Imagine!) I later discovered, and I've never forgotten, that correct last line in *Amazing Grace*. I know the word I had always sung as "we" has an "apostrophe d." This may be unimportant to others, but it was a devastating experience for me, and to this day, I still remember how I felt that day. My mother's counsel was to claim Romans 8:28. I know I cried on her shoulder.

Next stop: Baylor. And a word about my brother Johnny, who died on June 11, 1979, of emphysema from years of smoking. I loved Johnny. He was good to me, and later on he was good to my children. He was a great guy. I was so proud to be his brother.

Johnny Reynolds played professional football with the Chicago Cardinals, and in those days football players were not paid much money. Johnny was paid maybe $200 a game, which was a lot of money then, but nothing compared to today's standards. We went to see some of the games. Remember, I had a railroad pass.

Johnny played several years, but it was because of his many football injuries that he was unable to serve or disqualified from going into the service during World War II. Plus the fact that he was married and had a little girl named Carol (who now lives in Dallas and is married to Tommy Keele). Johnny belonged to the Masons and after he earned his 32nd degree, he became very involved in the Shrine in Dallas. He later became potentate of his Shrine unit.

Baylor 1

Baylor was a blast! I loved it. I went to class from 8 to 12, five days a week. Every afternoon from 1 to 5, I worked as a driver of a garbage truck. That, plus my summer jobs, paid my way through school. Many weekends I used my railroad pass and went home to Tyler. It was a three-hour train ride, and I used that travel time to study.

The usual things happened at Baylor. I made a lot of friends. I'm proud to say I still have many of those friends, but, sadly, I've also outlived quite a few. And then in September of 1941 I entered law school. I loved it. I had great professors, great fellow students, and it all fell into place. Dean Jackson became my very good friend, and Judge Joe Hale, a distinguished judge on the Waco Court of Appeals, was my mentor and friend. He taught Practice Court at Baylor and, without being a braggart, I ate it up.

But something happened in December '41 that changed the world and changed my life: Japan attacked Pearl Harbor.

I had just turned 20. I thought about enlisting and helping with the war effort, but both Dean Jackson and Judge Hale said "no." So I doubled up my classes and continued in law school even through the summer, as there was no summer vacation.

In the fall of 1942 I was sitting in chapel, where we attended every school day. A young Marine, fresh from Guadalcanal, the first battle in the Pacific, was our chapel speaker. He walked out on the stage on crutches, wearing his dress blues, and looking like a movie actor. He had medals all over his chest. He made a short talk about how it was on Guadalcanal and ended his speech with these words:

"If any of you young men want to kill Japs, meet me outside."

I was the first in line. I joined the Marine Corps and was told to stay in law school until I was called to active duty. In the interim, I went to Dallas, Texas, where I had to take a physical to be sure that I qualified. And I stood in line that day with several people whose lives would become interwoven with mine. I knew none of these boys; they didn't know me; but we were to become lifelong friends.

One was George Cire, a student at St. Edward's in Austin, who was originally from Houston. Another was Dick Davis, from the University of Texas, but originally from Houston. A third was Tom Berry, from the University of Texas, but at that time the son of the commanding general of the Texas National Guard, living in Austin.

I passed the physical, went back to law school, and worked like a Trojan, but I still drove the garbage truck in the afternoons. I finished my first year of law school. I did well. By doubling up, I finished my second year of law school and did well.

Then on July 1, 1943, I was told, along with some other Baylor boys who had joined the Marines and passed their physicals, that we were to report to Southwestern University in Georgetown, Texas, for further education before going to boot camp.

At this juncture I'm tempted to reflect back on those three years at Baylor and tell you about all my personal experiences. But my better judgment tells me not to do that. For the sake of people with orange blood, I will say that in the spring of 1942 I had the privilege of escorting the Baylor Princess to Texas University Spring Roundup. Beppy and Papa John helped me buy a tux and all that kind of stuff in order to escort this girl, whose name, if I can remember, was Mary Farrow, who happened to be the cousin of Anita Farrow, whom I later met as Susie Stamper's roommate—later—a war later.

At Southwestern, I took courses in Physics, Celestial Navigation, Calculus, Mechanical Drawing, and Obstacle Course Running. I was there four months in school, with all of the football players from the University of Texas, Baylor, TCU, SMU, and other Southwest Conference schools. This was called the V-12 Program.

In late October, some of us were selected to go to boot camp. It was a train ride very unlike the ones I had taken to St. Louis as a boy.

On an extremely hot fall day, I arrived at a place called Parris Island, South Carolina. Somebody called it "The Land That God Forgot." My introduction to boot camp was unbelievable. My drill instructor (DI) was a redneck from Tennessee by the name of John Casalle. He hated anyone who had ever been to college. I was immediately given the name of "Educated *.* [expletive] [expletive]."

Everyone's experiences in boot camp were pretty much the same. You can read about them in any book and they would all apply to me. However, two events stand out in my memory. On the third day in boot camp, on a Sunday afternoon following an inedible meal, DI Casalle made us fall out with packs and two canteens full of water. We marched to the beach and then we were told to take our entrenching tool and fill our packs with sand having an estimated weight of 80 pounds.

Then the 500 Marines of Platoon 828 were ordered to take a forced march of 26 miles. It was blazing hot. The sun was bearing down, and we were told that we would finish before 7 p.m. We all started out jovially, laughingly, and confidently. By 4 o'clock in the afternoon, things had changed. In fact, a lot of my friends had either fallen out, passed out, or quit. But a word: if you didn't finish, you would never be considered for candidate's class, or what the Army calls OCS. By 5 o'clock, I could see the blood from the blisters on my feet, and I wasn't sure that I would finish.

Sometime later, I saw Casalle maybe 200 yards in front of me, not carrying a pack, yelling that we had only a short distance to go, and that our goal was to reach the ocean. Marching with me were two friends from Baylor and Southwestern, one by the name of Jack Jones, whom we called "Lone," and another guy from Baylor, a big football player named Tuffy McCormick.

Half a mile from the ocean, I knew I was going to faint. Lone Jones whispered to me that he couldn't make it, at which point the big

SCHOOL YEARS

old boy behind us by the name of Tuffy reached over and took each of our packs, and said, "We'll make it together," and carried three packs for half a mile. He gave me back my pack and gave Lone his, and the three of us reached the Atlantic Ocean together.

But that is not the incident that changed my life. On the 16th day of boot camp, we had an official inspection of all the remaining Marines in Platoon 828, along with our lieutenant and Casalle, who were inspecting each of us with a fine-tooth comb. While inspecting our rifles, they would ask us a military question and we were graded on the basis of how we handled that inspection.

As the lieutenant came to me, he grabbed my rifle while I was standing at rigid attention. Then he asked me the toughest military question I'd ever been asked or had ever dreamed of, when he asked me the question: "What is a loose piece?" I had never heard of anything like that. From somewhere on the dark side of my nature, I said, "Sir, a loose piece is a prostitute" to which the lieutenant said, "Well, I'll be damned. Take his name."

When boot camp was over and they called the roll of the class, I was Number One. I, and along with 12 others, including Buddy Berry, Tuffy McCormick, Les Proctor, and John Quay, were sent to Quantico to train to be officers in the United States Marine Corps.

Which brings us to **The War Years**.

CHAPTER 3

The War Years

My introduction to Quantico was interesting. Quantico is the place where they train Marine officers. It has a wonderful history, it is a beautiful base, and it is located at Triangle, Virginia. I was fortunate and honored to be there. On my very first day, we marched to an auditorium and, seated in very comfortable theater seats, about 200 of us became wide awake when a full colonel by the name of Fay walked on the stage of the auditorium.

His remarks were short. After telling us that there was a little old school on the Hudson (West Point) and another off of the Chesapeake Bay (the Naval Academy), we had the special privilege of attending the greatest military training school in the world-*i.e.*, Quantico, Virginia. A few minutes later he closed his speech by telling us to look at the man on our left and to look at the man on our right, and that when this war was over, one of those men would not come back. Of course he was right. (Later I ran into Colonel Fay on Iwo Jima and reminded him that so far, I had made it.)

I was surprised to learn that Marine Corps strategy was almost a carbon copy of the tactics used by Stonewall Jackson in the War Between the States. The Marine Corps adopted and used what was described to us as the Triangle Division, which meant each division had three regiments, each regiment had three battalions, each battalion had three companies, each company had three platoons, and each platoon had three squads.

The "tactics of the triangle" are very flexible and well adapted to infantry maneuvers. This entire concept copied Jackson's great brigade as well as his epic conduct of the Second Battle of Manassas. Incidentally, the Marine Corps still uses the Triangle Division, modified to some degree by the tactics used by Fox Company, Seventh Marines, led by Captain Bill Barber at the Battle of the Chosin Reservoir in North Korea (discussed later in this book).

My days at Quantico were successful. I had found my niche. I lived and breathed the Marine Corps. However, during this time frame I had another experience that would greatly influence my life. One weekend I went to Washington, D.C., 30 miles away, to meet two of my friends from Tyler: Bob Payne and Talmadge Main. Bob was in the Navy and Talmadge was in the Army. We had been friends during my Tyler years and the three of us had gone to junior college in Tyler together.

On the weekend that we met in Washington, unlike most others, we decided to go to church on Sunday morning. Talmadge was a Presbyterian, Bob was a Baptist, and I was a Methodist. We decided that we would get in a cab there at our hotel and ask the taxi driver to drive us to the nearest Presbyterian, Baptist, or Methodist church. This nice man said, "You don't need my taxi. There's a Presbyterian church next to the hotel here, and you can see the people standing in line ready to enter church." We walked less than 50 yards and stood in line to go to church. I had never before stood in line to go to church.

While we were standing there, a man came by with his wife and saw the three of us in uniform, each from a different branch of the

THE WAR YEARS

service, and asked us if we would like to sit with him and his wife, and afterwards have lunch. He introduced himself as Judge Lynch of the Washington Court of Appeals. We sat with Judge and Mrs. Lynch in the upper balcony overlooking the pulpit. The church was crowded. And incidentally, this was the church Abraham Lincoln attended while he was President. In fact, Judge Lynch pointed out Lincoln's regular pew, which was slightly slanted so as to accommodate his height. After the preliminaries, a man stood up and preached, and I had never heard such a preacher. This man was Dr. Peter Marshall.

I was so impressed that, after having lunch with the judge and his wife, and saying goodbye to my friends, I stayed in Washington to go to the evening service. Prior to the service, I met Dr. Marshall and that was the beginning of a beautiful friendship. Thereafter, I tried to attend New York Avenue Presbyterian Church every Sunday that I was at Quantico.

After I went overseas, Dr. Marshall was good enough to send me copies of his sermons, and I was smart enough to preserve them. Not long ago, Susie found the few remaining sermons I had left and Carol put them into book form. Of course, this is one of my life's treasures. If you as a reader have a thirst for God's tremendous word, look for the little book of Peter Marshall's sermons found somewhere on my bookshelf.

Meanwhile, back at Quantico: I learned the art of combat, and after approximately six months, I was one of the fortunate few to be promoted to a second lieutenant. I was then assigned to artillery school at Quantico, so as to prepare me to become a forward observer and to run a fire direction center in combat. I learned how to direct the artillery fire of 75-pack Howitzers, 105 Howitzers, and 155 Howitzers. (Howitzers are commonly called cannons, which are assigned to infantry to support attacks by laying down artillery barrages so as to assist the infantry attack enemy defenses.) This training was very intensive and involved how to estimate distances, angles of fire, various types of targets, and the type of projectiles needed to destroy the enemy or to block their vision of our movements.

Following graduation from artillery school, I was given orders to join the Third Marine Division, Twelfth Marines (the artillery regiment), in the South Pacific. The year was 1944, and the Battle of Saipan in the Central Pacific was about to start.

I went aboard ship, along with other replacements, and joined up with the Third Marine Division at a giant lagoon at Eniwetok, an atoll of the Marshall Islands in the Central Pacific. The Third Marine Division was in reserve for the Battle of Saipan. I remained aboard ship in that lagoon for 49 days, waiting for word as to when we would land. Of course, the word changed. Instead of going into Saipan, the Third Marine Division made an amphibious landing on the Island of Guam in the Central Pacific, where I first met the Japanese in person. I was a green forward observer.

The Third Marine Division had just left Bougainville in the Solomon Islands, and I was the new kid on the block. It didn't take long to learn.

Rather than give a detailed, day-by-day account of our tramping through the jungles of Guam and trying to find clean water mingled with the bodies of dead Japs killed by our artillery fire, let me just say that the Marines easily wiped out the Japanese and returned the island of Guam to the good old USA. (To this day, I don't like to be in a jungle-like atmosphere or area.) At the close of the campaign, Guam became the headquarters of Admiral Nimitz and the U.S. Pacific Fleet. Guam also became the base camp of the Third Marine Division.

THE WAR YEARS

Two nonmilitary experiences of WWII are worth noting. The first has to do with Christmas Eve 1944, after the campaign of Guam had been for all intents and purposes completed. The Twelfth Marines were camped on the east side of Guam approximately 20 miles from the town of Agaña. A friend of mine, a second lieutenant from Long Island, New York, told me that Navy personnel from some of the ships berthed in Agaña harbor were going to perform on Christmas Eve, starting at 6 p.m., *The Messiah*. I was not familiar with *The Messiah*, but Ted assured me that we needed to go, since we were excused from training Christmas Eve and Christmas.

The only problem was that we had no way to get there. So the two of us walked some 20 miles to hear this beautiful music. It was great. It made a profound impression upon me, and I have never forgotten it. When a Navy nurse with the most beautiful voice I had ever heard sang that great soprano solo, "Come Unto Me," it touched my heart. The performance ended around 9 o'clock or later that night, and Ted and I had the problem of getting back to camp. Fortunately, some Navy officer knew that we had walked to get there and was good enough to have us driven back to our camp.

The second experience occurred on Christmas Day. While I was recuperating from the walk, about 9:30 that morning, a young Marine from Temple, Texas, named Keifer Marshall, drove up in a Jeep and asked for Lieutenant Reynolds. He came into our tent, and I introduced myself to him. He told me that General Erskine, the commanding general of the Third Marine Division, had sent him to pick me up with my sea bag, because I was being transferred that day to the Second Marine Division stationed on the island of Saipan, 90 miles north of the island of Guam.

Keifer took me to General Erskine's tent that Christmas morning with my mind whirling over what was going on. I had never met General Erskine. As a matter of fact, I was afraid that I was in deep trouble. But when I went into his tent, he told me to sit down, that he wanted to talk to me.

He told me that he had learned that my brother Earl had been in a B-29 accident at Saipan, when a plane exploded as it landed on its return from bombing Tokyo, while Earl was removing the bomb site. The bomb sites on the B-29s were very precious and were treated like fine diamonds. Earl was responsible for inserting and dismantling these bomb sites before and on landing from bomb runs. General Erskine told me that Earl was severely burned, was not expected to live, and that he was transferring me to Saipan with the Second Marine Division, so that I could spend with Earl the last days of his life.

Keifer took me to the Naval Airport, and I was put aboard a C-47 and flown to Saipan. While flying, I wondered but was never told how General Erskine knew about Earl. I wondered if any other Marine officer had ever had the opportunity of such a transfer as mine. I never heard of another.

We arrived on Saipan. A Jeep met me, and I was taken to Second Marine Division headquarters, assigned to a tent, then taken to the Army hospital, where I found my brother Earl wrapped in bandages from head to toe. For the next six days I sat with Earl, talking and crying and praying, and living out what I thought were his last days.

On January 1, I was flown back to Guam. Keifer met me at the airport and I was taken back to Able Battery, Twelfth Marines, from whence I had come. It was not until some time later, after I returned back to Guam from duty at Iwo Jima, and a stay at a hospital in Hawaii, that I learned that Earl had made it and had been transferred to a hospital at Fort Bliss, El Paso, Texas.

Earl was severely scarred, and he never married because of it. He came back from the war, graduated from Texas A&M with a civil engineering degree, and came to Houston, where his life for the next almost 40 years was closely interwoven with that of Susie, Hunt, Dan, and me. He was a great brother, brilliant and gifted, but full of complexes because of his disfigured face, which none of us ever noticed.

Iwo Jima

Shortly after February 1, 1945, the Third Marine Division went aboard ship, destination Iwo Jima. The Fourth and Fifth Marine Divisions, with the Fourth on the right and the Fifth near Mount Suribachi, landed abreast on the eastern shore of Iwo on February 19, 1945. Once again, the Third Marine Division was in reserve. That doesn't mean we didn't go ashore. Until the 22nd of February, we unloaded Navy ships taking ammunition from landing craft to the landing beaches, and on D-Day the 19th, my job was to haul 105 Howitzer shells to both landing beaches for the Fourth and Fifth Divisions.

On D-Day, 50 yards onshore, I ran into my friend Dick Davis, the second lieutenant from Houston, Texas, with whom I'd stood in line in Dallas the day I joined the Marine Corps. It was a brief but happy reunion. My landing craft made many trips to and from the ammunition ships to the ammunition depot we established on the beaches.

The beaches were under constant attack by Japanese artillery, firing from the central part of Iwo, from positions north of the second airstrip. The Japs had zeroed in on the beaches and, except for our own naval gunfire and naval planes, all of us would have been blown sky-high. The Fifth Marines pushed in a considerable distance, but the Fourth Marines couldn't budge. It lasted this way for several days, and then on the 22nd, the Third Division-my division-was given the responsibility to land and pass through the center between the Fourth and Fifth Divisions. It wasn't fun.

It was on the first airstrip, either the first or second day we were ashore, that I looked up to the top of Suribachi and saw a very small American flag flying at the top. It was clearly recognizable. Sometime later that same day, a larger flag replaced the small one, and the Stars and Stripes proudly waved as an inspiration to all of us on Iwo Jima and to the American people forever. But I didn't have time to keep my eyes on the flag very long. And I sure didn't appreciate that this would become one of the most recognizable art subjects in the world.

Seeing that flag atop Suribachi stirred my emotions to the core. We paused, looked back, and tears came to our eyes. That flag represented America and was what I was fighting for. To you it may be corny, but to the day I die, I will see within my heart the American flag waving atop Mount Suribachi.

Sometime in the '90s, a talk show host was belittling Congress's attempt to make burning the American flag illegal. As I listened, I got madder and madder. I finally stopped my car and composed a letter to the radio station, lamenting the lack of appreciation for the many Americans who had died for that flag.

At Iwo, we were told to "Attack and Take" the second airstrip in the center of the island. This airstrip ran north and south, as I remember, and it was approximately 400 yards from where we were dug in to our objective north of the airstrip. That objective consisted of small hills riddled with caves filled with Japs armed to the teeth.

Crossing this flat strip of land was no picnic. The enemy was looking down our throats, and they could clearly see what we were doing. I need to repeat: *They were looking down our throats*. And we couldn't see theirs. Our artillery fired smoke shells masking the Japs' view, and the First Battalion of the Ninth Marines of the Third Marine Division, to which I was attached as forward observer, was told to

"Move Out" at high port-or on a dead run-in an attempt to reach various shell holes in the airstrip for protection.

We did not make it across on the first day. Several things happened that first night as we dug in on Airstrip Number Two. The first I remember is that our ammunition dump was blown to smithereens, and I thought the island of Iwo was going to break apart. If you dug one foot below the surface into the volcanic sand that covered this island, it was hot with heat from the volcano that was Suribachi. As a matter of fact, in order to even lie down on the ground, you had to put a poncho under you to keep your body from blistering.

But as the inferno from the explosion waned, it began to rain in torrents, and the rain was very cold. Seeing a Japanese airplane wing lying ten feet from the shell hole where I was dug in, I crawled over to the wrecked wing and managed to drag it to my hole and pulled it across the hole as a roof to keep out the rain. This was a huge mistake. In a matter of minutes, a Japanese mortar shell struck the airplane wing, and both of my legs from the knees down were filled with shrapnel splinters of aluminum from my "roof." I now had heat not only coming from below but these aluminum splinters were like pieces of fire. Guess where I thought I was!

Within an hour or two, daylight came, and our smoke shells blocked the vision of the Japs, so we continued our attack to the caves across the airstrip. This time we made it. The company, Able Company, Ninth Marines, to which I was attached, suffered 128 percent casualties, as many were hit twice, crossing the second airstrip. We were lucky. This is where Admiral Chester Nimitz coined the term that at Iwo, "uncommon valor was a common virtue."

From the taking of the second airstrip till the end of the campaign, the rest of the battle has been duly chronicled by many writers, all more scholarly and gifted than I. But I'll just say that the Battle of Iwo Jima involved hand-to-hand combat, face-to-face with a determined enemy, and that my role was to direct artillery fire on the enemy from my forward position. We were under constant fire. But we took Iwo Jima in what has been described as one of the bloodiest battles of Marine Corps history, and that little island became one of our greatest assets in prosecuting the War in the Pacific. This little island became a haven for crippled planes returning from bombing runs over Japan as they made their way back to safety.

On one occasion, General Erskine ordered a night attack and Able Company, Ninth Marines, was able to advance in this dead of night less than a hundred yards, while Baker Company to our right advanced several hundred yards, and Charlie Company to Baker's right hardly moved at all. Morning found Baker Company out in front by several hundred yards, *totally surrounded by Japs*. We couldn't reach them, and they were having a hard time getting back to us.

It was at this time that I saw my friend Jack Leims pick up a Marine and put him on his shoulder, and bring that Marine from Baker Company's position back to our position. After leaving his buddy, Jack made this trip again and again and again, while we stood helpless, watching my friend Jack, the company commander of Baker Company, rescue his wounded buddies.

After the war, Jack and I would meet again and, as fate would have it, I became his lawyer. Jack was awarded the Medal of Honor, and hanging on my wall is a gold-embossed recreation of that famous flag-planting at Iwo Jima, on which Jack inscribed, *"To my brother in arms, Joe Reynolds,"* and further quoting those great lines from *Henry V*:

> *We few, we happy few, we band of brothers. He who sheds his blood with me this day is my brother.*

THE WAR YEARS

Several days later, some Marine told me that there was a platoon commander from the Fifth Marine Division on our left, who was asking for me. I crawled over to the Fifth's position, where I met my friend George Cire. George told me that after I had left the beach on D-Day, he learned that our friend Dick Davis had been killed. Several days later still, after meeting with George, I was told that George had been shot twice and evacuated to a hospital in Hawaii. Little did I know that in several weeks I would be in the hospital with him.

The battle progressed at a snail's pace and was very costly, until we finally reached the northern end of the island. I can only say that Japs were entrenched in every cave and we had to rout 'em and burn 'em out, and that was a tough thing for this 23-year-old to do. When we had finally cleaned up the island of Japs, I went back to the foot of Suribachi. I could see that Star-Spangled Banner. What this symbolized to me, and still symbolizes today, is that the Star-Spangled Banner still waves *over the land of the free and the home of the brave.*

After we won that Battle of Iwo Jima and secured the island for the USA and her allies, things happened very fast. We had no sooner taken the airstrip than the Seabees came in and filled up the shell holes. And the very next day brought B-29s returning from raids on Tokyo to the airstrip to land their damaged planes. Thousands of lives were saved by having these runways on this small but valuable volcanic island in the Pacific.

But on that day when I met George Cire, my legs were swollen and infected, and I looked like a pin cushion. Before we left the island, though, I happened to walk upon an amazing scene: that of seeing the Marine cemetery and thousands of white crosses, with a Jewish chaplain dedicating the graves and invoking Almighty God's protection, not only for the surviving Marines but also for the souls of my departed friends. This experience is by far the most lasting impression I have of Iwo Jima. The scene haunts me. And try as I may, I can't erase it from my mind.

For a long time I had a copy of the words spoken by the rabbi, but somewhere over the years I lost it, or perhaps it was just misplaced and went to one of those secret places where lost things go until they want to be found. I strongly remember that those words were appropriate for all of them. After the service, I looked for the grave of Dick Davis, but I couldn't find it. There were just too many crosses.

Shortly after first writing the above passage, I had the privilege of appearing on Ed Hendee's talk show on Houston's radio station KSEV 700 AM. It was Memorial Day 2001. At the conclusion of the interview, Ed asked me what was my most memorable experience in World War II. I recited to Ed this very emotional experience that happened that morning at the dedication of the cemetery. I also explained my deep regret at having lost those beautiful words of the rabbi.

Believe it or not, a former Marine listening to the program called me and told me with a trembling voice, "I have a copy and I'll send it to you tomorrow, provided you take me to lunch sometime before the summer is over." It is with joy that I attach to this story the remarks from the dedication by Chaplain Roland B. Gittelsohn at the cemetery at the foot of Suribachi:

> **The PUREST DEMOCRACY**
> **Sermon on the Dedication of 5th Marine Division Cemetery on Iwo Jima**
> **By Chaplain Roland B. Gittelsohn**
>
> *THIS IS PERHAPS THE GRIMMEST, and surely the holiest, task we have faced since D-Day. Here before us lie the bodies of comrades and friends. Men who until yesterday or last week laughed with us,*

trained with us. Men who were on the same ships with us, and went over the sides with us, as we prepared to hit the beaches of this island. Men who fought with us and feared with us. Somewhere in this plot of ground there may lie the man who could have discovered the cure for cancer. Under one of these Christian crosses, or beneath a Jewish Star of David, there may rest now a man who was destined to be a great prophet to find the way, perhaps, for all to live in plenty, with poverty and hardship for none. Now they lie here silently in this sacred soil, and we gather to consecrate this earth in their memory.

IT IS NOT EASY TO DO SO. Some of us have buried our closest friends here. We saw these men killed before our very eyes. Any one of us might have died in their places. Indeed, some of us are alive and breathing at this very moment only because men who lie here beneath us had the courage and strength to give their lives for ours. To speak in memory of such men as these is not easy, Of these, too, can it be said with utter truth: "The world will little note nor long remember what we say here. It can never forget what they did here."

No, our poor power of speech can add nothing to what these men and the other dead of our division who are not here have already done. All that we can even hope to do is follow their example. To show the same selfless courage in peace that they did in war. To swear that, by the grace of God and the stubborn strength and power of human will, their sons and ours shall never suffer these pains again. These men have done their job well. They have paid the ghastly price of freedom. If that freedom be once again lost, as it was after the last war, the unforgivable blame will be ours, not theirs. So it be the living who are here to be dedicated and consecrated.

WE DEDICATE OURSELVES, first, to live together in peace the way they fought and are buried in war. Here lie men who loved America because their ancestors, generations ago, helped in her founding, and other men who loved her with equal passion, because they themselves or their own fathers escaped from oppression to her blessed shores.

Here lie officers and men, Negroes and whites, rich men and poor . . . together. Here are Protestants, Catholics, and Jews . . . together. Here no man prefers another because of his faith or despises him because of his color. Here there are no quotas of how many from each group are admitted or allowed. Among these men there is no discrimination. No prejudice. No hatred. Theirs is the highest and purest democracy.

Any man among us, the living, who fails to understand that, will thereby betray those who lie here dead. Whoever of us lifts his hand in hate against a brother, or thinks himself superior to those who happen to be in the minority, makes of this ceremony and of the bloody sacrifice it commemorates, an empty, hollow mockery. To this, then, as our solemn, sacred duty, do we the living now dedicate ourselves: to the right of Protestants, Catholics, and Jews, of white men and Negroes alike, to enjoy the democracy for which all of them have here paid the price.

TO ONE THING MORE do we consecrate ourselves in memory of those who sleep beneath these crosses and stars. We shall not foolishly suppose, as did the last generation of America's fighting men, that victory on the battlefield will automatically guarantee the triumph of democracy at home. This war, with all its frightful heartache and suffering, is but the beginning of our generation's struggle for democracy. When the last battle has been won, there will be those at home, as there were last time, who will want us to turn our backs in selfish isolation on the rest of organized humanity, and thus to sabotage the very peace for which we fight. We promise you who lie here: we will not do that. We will join hands with Britain, China, Russia-in peace, even as we have in war, to build the kind of world for which you died.

WHEN THE LAST SHOT has been fired, there will still be those eyes that are turned backward-not forward-who will be satisfied with those wide extremes of poverty and wealth in which the seeds of another war can breed. We promise you, our departed comrades: this, too, we will

THE WAR YEARS

not permit. This war has been fought by the common man; its fruits of peace must be enjoyed by the common man. We promise, by all that is sacred and holy, that your sons, the sons of miners and millers, the sons of farmers and workers, will inherit from your death the right to a living that is decent and secure.

WHEN THE FINAL CROSS has been placed in the last cemetery, once again there will be those to whom profit is more important than peace, who will insist with the voice of sweet reasonableness and appeasement that it is better to trade with the enemies of mankind, than, by crushing them, to lose their profit. To you who sleep here silently, we give our promise: we will not listen. We will not forget that some of you were burnt with oil that came from American wells, that many of you were killed by shells fashioned from American steel. We promise that when once again men seek profit at your expense, we shall remember how you looked when we placed you reverently, lovingly, in the ground.

THUS DO WE MEMORIALIZE those who, having ceased living with us, now live within us. Thus do we consecrate ourselves, the living, to carry on the struggle they began. Too much blood has gone into this soil for us to let it lie barren. Too much pain and heartache have fertilized the earth on which we stand. We here solemnly swear: this shall not be in vain. Out of this, and from the suffering and sorrow of those who mourn this, will come-we promise-the birth of a new freedom for the sons of men everywhere. AMEN.

There are other incidents that occurred at Iwo. Like the time a Jap crawled into my foxhole at night, only to be killed by my buddy, Freddie Doll, whom we called "Paper." When this Jap slid into our foxhole, I was asleep. Paper was on watch, and he merely strangled the Jap to death. I woke up, knowing it was not a dream.

Or there was this time this young Marine captured a Jap, which was a very rare experience. And he told Major Glass, the battalion commander of First Battalion, Ninth Marines, that he had him. And Major Glass told this boy, "I don't have time right now to fool with you or the prisoner. You take care of him." An hour or two later, Major Glass said to me, "Find that boy and that prisoner." I found the boy, told him the major wanted to see him and the prisoner, and the boy looked at me sheepishly, and said, "I took care of him." I never told Major Glass. I told the boy to get back to his unit.

Another Iwo Jima story occurred 50 years later: I was sitting at the Texas Club, having lunch with two Marine friends of mine, both of whom are named Joe Reynolds! We had been at Iwo together and we had been in Korea together. And while we talked, I told the two Joes that I had a brilliant idea, and I asked the waiter to bring me a phone, which he did. I called a former Marine by the name of Lynn Ashby, then Editor of the now-defunct *Houston Post*, and told Lynn that I would like to be sent by the *Post* back for the 50th Anniversary of the landing on Iwo Jima, so that I could send back daily reports on how things were at Iwo in this modern day, as compared to 50 years before. Lynn said he thought it was a great idea, but that he would have to get permission and would call me back.

About 20 minutes later, Lynn called back to the restaurant and told me that he was sorry, but the *Post* said no. I told him I understood, and it was just an idea. He then asked me if I would like to know why they weren't sending me? I said, "yeah, I would like to know." And he said to me, "*I'm* going." Turned out he didn't get to go, but my friend Johnny Baker went, and he brought back to me a test tube filled with black sand from the beaches of Iwo Jima. It too is one of my treasured possessions.

As we boarded ship leaving Iwo, we were only a few days out to sea when this old and dilapidated ship on which we were sailing ran into a typhoon that nearly sank us! It was so bad. The ship's name was the *Santa Isabella*, and we said it must have been the

THE WAR YEARS

sister ship to the *Santa Maria*, Columbus's ship to America. Vinnie Robinson and I shared the same bunk area. He had the upper bunk and I had the lower bunk, because I couldn't climb. But it didn't make any difference, because the ship rolled and pitched so badly, there was no way to sleep.

And eating was out of the question. If you went to the mess hall, the food would go from one end of the table to the other with every lurch of the ship. I've often wished that I had had the upper bunk, because on the lower bunk, when Vinnie got seasick, there was no way I could escape from all that stuff that kept coming out of his mouth. I finally moved on deck and watched the waves come crashing over the ship. But that beat the stench and the crud from Vinnie's and my bunk room.

When we landed back at Guam, the doctor took one look at my legs and ordered me to Hawaii. By that time, I had squeezed most of the Japanese metal splinters out of my legs, but some were embedded and I couldn't remove them. It was then that I wound up in the hospital next to George Cire, and in a few days I was back to normal. George had been shot in the stomach and was unable to walk. I spent those few days sitting with him. It was during this stay in the hospital that a young Marine PFC, as I recall, George's friend, came to see him on his way to Guam. His name was Joe Jamail. Joe is another one of those people who became a part of my life along with George. More later.

Before I left the hospital, I came down with dengue fever and worse than all the shrapnel, and worse than the rocking *Santa Isabella*, was this horrible fever that literally decked me and made me wish for pleasant days at battle with the Japs looking down our throats on Iwo.

One last note about World War II. After recuperating from the effects of Iwo Jima, the Third Marine Division was ordered aboard ship, destination Japan. It was during the time of our loading of the ships, headed for Japan, that we learned that America had dropped an atomic bomb on Japan at Hiroshima. And then we heard about the second bomb at Nagasaki and that the war had ended.

I want to say this about the atomic bomb. Don't ask me if it was the right thing to do. I resent that question. I can state with total certainty that thousands of my friends, and perhaps I, would have died on the beaches of Japan, had it not been for the atomic bomb. I owe my life to that bomb, and so do thousands of other Marines. It makes me sick to hear these modern-day clowns discuss a subject they know nothing about.

I've had a very hard time forgiving the Japs. They mistreated prisoners more so than did the Nazis in their concentration camps. They were evil and bent on destroying not only America but my friends and me. I remember Pearl Harbor. But I exaggerate my bitterness. There are evildoers and evilmongers in every society and in every race. Truthfully, I have learned not to judge people by race, color, or creed, but as individuals.

However, I still don't eat at Japanese restaurants, and I don't drive Japanese cars.

And I still salute the American flag.

CHAPTER 4

Joe, Susie, Hunt, and Dan

I fell in love with Susie the first time I saw her. It was truly love at first sight, from my point of view only. She was in her heyday at Baylor: President of Alpha Omega, Honor Society, and everything that had a president, and she had boyfriends galore! All I had were some old khaki clothes and a worn-out Plymouth Charger that my sister had given me. In addition, I had no job, no money, and I had a long way to go. She wouldn't give me the time of day. She didn't know me, and she didn't *want* to know me. But it's funny how things change.

I didn't give up. When she wouldn't return my calls, I went home to Tyler one weekend and cried on my mother's shoulder, and-since she hated to see a grown boy cry-she came up with a marvelous idea of my making a long distance call to Susie Stamper at Burleson Hall, Baylor. My mother even agreed to pay for the telephone call. Believe it or not, it worked; Susie took my call. I finally conned her into having a date, but I had to agree to make it a triple date, *i.e.*, two other couples had to go with us. She didn't trust Marines.

As Susie mentions in her reminiscences, on this first real date I told her that I was going to marry her. That statement did not go over very well. This was in the fall of the year, and six months later, things were no better for me. By this time she knew my first name, and every now and then she would take my call.

Sometime in March 1947 I took the bar exam and passed. On the day I passed, I was offered two jobs: one as a briefing attorney at the Supreme Court of Texas at $75 a month, and the other as an Assistant Attorney General of Texas at $300 a month. I figured with $300 a month, possibly I could get married, if I could overcome the resistance of the blonde bomber. It took a long time. I was finally at the point of nearly giving up, when I was in Houston one weekend, having been invited to a beach party at one of her friend's beach houses. Susie had invited me to be her date. By this time, I was a full-fledged lawyer-at least I had a license.

On the occasion of the beach party, I got sunburned badly. Everybody was trying to help. When she agreed to put salve, lotion, medicine, or whatever it was on my back, she obviously felt sorry for me. In this weakened state of mind, I sprung the question, "Would you consider going to California with me in July for two weeks in the Marine Corps at Camp Pendleton?" She startled me with a "yes." But it was subject to conditions: could her mother and daddy get ready for a wedding in six weeks?

In those days, taking a trip together meant being married, and this was my way of proposing, and she took it as such. This was no "lost weekend" deal; it was the real thing. The wedding itself was fabulous. It occurred at South Main Baptist Church in Houston. Everybody was there, and we left at midnight in a new Ford car I had just bought to drive to California. This meant a month-long trip. Somewhere among our souvenirs is a picture book of the two of us traveling to and from California by way of all the scenic sights between Houston and there, with notations at the bottom of each snapshot stating in some detail where we were and what was going on. All in all, it was a fabulous trip, and it was the beginning of a beautiful marriage. I have never regretted it one day.

JOE, SUSIE, HUNT, AND DAN

We lived in Austin, in a beautiful old duplex on Rio Grande, properly marked as a Texas historical place (but not because it was our honeymoon cottage). Our days there were wonderful. I traveled throughout the state trying lawsuits Joe Greenhill assigned to me, and in less than a year I had tried some 20 jury cases. Never has a young man been so lucky as I. Susie went with me on my trips, and we rode together across Texas-not on cowboy ponies, but in our new Ford car. As I tried lawsuits, she became the best-read person in the state. She went through novels as I went through a trial. We had fun.

While we were still living in Austin, Susie became pregnant, and we were hoping for a little boy. She would pick the name of a boy, and she did. Had it been a girl, I wanted her name to be Lillie Pearl. That did not go over with Susie. She said "no way."

While I was trying a case in Brownwood, Texas, Susie was staying with her parents in Houston. She called me by phone to tell me that she was going to the hospital. This was two weeks earlier than we had anticipated. I was staying in Brownwood with my friend Bill Alcorn and his wife, and when I got the news, Bill, who was the county attorney, finished the trial for me, and I caught the Santa Fe to Houston. Hunt was born on Susie's birthday, August 7, 1949. He was quite a boy. He still is.

Sometime in the fall of 1949, soon after Hunt was born, Fentress Bracewell called me and asked me to come to work in Houston at the firm of Bracewell & Tunks. Susie loved the idea of moving back to Houston. She had her family and her friends there. I thought it was the biggest place I'd ever seen outside of New York City. I was a small-town boy. But her family, the Stampers, were great people and my strongest supporters. It would be totally unfair and unjust for me not to add that both her mother and daddy aided my career in a thousand ways, not the least of which was telling their friends that I was the greatest young lawyer in the world. And they really believed it. Susie knew better, but she didn't like to argue with her parents. I knew better, too, but I kept quiet.

Seriously, the Stampers opened doors for me that would remain open for my entire legal career, and without them, the little success I've enjoyed would have been much smaller.

Hunt

Hunt was the best-looking child I ever saw. Until he was grown, he would have passed for a poster boy on any national magazine cover. Not only was he a handsome young man, but he was gifted intellectually and he didn't have a lazy bone in his body.

Looking back on those years, they went by far too swiftly, but we had fun. Hunt was a colicky baby, which meant that he never slept through a full night. Each night one of us had the honor of walking Hunt. We really didn't mind too much. As a little boy, he was mischievous but fun, and I forgave him when at the age of four he put sand in the gasoline tank of the Chevrolet I had just bought when the old Ford played out. That car was never the same.

At age seven, Hunt started a never-ending career with athletics. Because of his strength, which he got from Daddy Bo (Susie's father), he was able to play Little League baseball before he was eight. He had natural talent. The Little League years were wonderful. It was during this time that Mike Stevens and Brent Hammond became a part of our lives. More later on Mike and Brent.

For six years we were very involved in Little League baseball. Hunt was always a star. He started off as a left-handed catcher, but by the time he went to the "major" league, he was playing first base, because he was left-handed. The night we dedicated the new Bob Smith Baseball Park on Westheimer, Hunt hit the first pitch out of the ball park, all the way to Westheimer! I let everyone know he was

JOE, SUSIE, HUNT, AND DAN

my son. I was so proud of him. He continued to hit like that for the three years in the "major leagues." He then played pony league ball, but his greatest accomplishments were in high school.

These same kids that he had started out with, in their senior year in high school, won the city championship, beating all the schools in the Houston School District, and then won the district title and the regional title, and went to the state championship playoffs in Austin. In the championship game against Corpus Christi, Lee High School lost 2 to 1. The pitcher for Corpus was a young boy by the name of Burt Hooton, who would later break into the major leagues with the Chicago Cubs and play many years of professional baseball as a right-handed pitcher for the Los Angeles Dodgers. As this is written, he is a pitching coach for the Round Rock Express, one of the Houston Astros' farm clubs.

But Hunt's participation in football was the most fun of all. Although he was small for a football player, again his strength made him a very good player. He was an offensive lineman and played extremely well. He lettered both years, and his senior year he was second string all-district. His high school coaches told me that if Hunt had been four inches taller and 40 pounds heavier, he would have been All-American in college. One of his coaches also told me that he had the highest IQ of any player he had ever coached. He didn't tell me what the number was.

DAN

Dan was born June 29, 1955, in Houston. We lived in the big white house on Stamper Way, in the home where Susie had grown up as a girl. We paid market value for the house. The Stampers lived next door in their mansion. Beppie came to stay with us to help Susie with Dan. That same year, Hunt started to school at Grady. The problem with living next door to the Stampers was that Hunt would come home from school and check both houses to see what each was having for dinner. He seldom ate with us.

◄ TOUCHED BY GRACE

Dan was a lovable child. Everything went right. By the time he was of school age, we had moved to our new home at 6226 Lynbrook in Tanglewood. It was-and still is-a beautiful home on a corner lot where still stand the live oak trees I myself planted. We made many wonderful memories while living at that house. An interesting story about that house is remembered in Chapter 6, but I need to get back on the subject, which is Dan.

Dan started to school at Second Baptist Church School. Dan's career followed the same history as Hunt's. He played Little League and participated in sports, but his heart was with horses.

One Sunday morning he begged me to take him to the Houston Livestock Show Rodeo to see the Quarter Horse Show. I had never been to one; neither had he. We played hooky from Sunday School, over Susie's objection, and found ourselves out at the "Domed Stadium." The Quarter Horse Show was awesome. There was a black stallion that was Grand Champion, and Dan and I thought it was the most beautiful horse in the world.

We went around to the stalls looking for the black stallion and found him. As we stood there, looking at the horse, a man in overalls walked up to me and asked if I was Mr. Reynolds with the Houston School Board. I said, "yes." He asked me about Dan. I told him that we had come to look at the black horse, because we had never seen anything that beautiful. He asked Dan if he had a horse. Dan said, "no."

This man introduced himself as Preacher O'Quinn and told me that he and his wife had followed my career with the school board through the years, and that I was one of their heroes. He then asked Dan, "Would you like to have a horse from a stallion better than the black horse?" And while I stuttered, Dan said, "yes." I protested, "We have no place to keep a horse. We know nothing about horses." He said, "That's no problem, I'll keep the horse at

JOE, SUSIE, HUNT, AND DAN

my ranch at the corner of Highway 6 and 290, and you can bring Dan to ride his horse every Saturday." We were now in the horse business.

In the meantime, Jennifer Walker, who lived at the corner of Voss and Memorial, taught Dan how to ride. He was a quick learner. He was a natural. In 1966, Helen Walker called me and told me they were moving to Fulshear, and since we needed a place to keep horses, they would like to sell us their home at the corner of Voss and Memorial, so Dan would have a place to keep his horse. What could I say? What could I do? We did purchase that property at Voss and Memorial, and live there to this day. But the rest of that story comes later, when I discuss the Mike Lallinger connection.

We have a dream home, thanks to its location, Helen's genius, and Susie's and Helen's gift of interior decoration. We are still making memories in this house on the northeast corner of Memorial and Voss in the midst of the "Memorial Villages" section of Houston, Texas.

Before Dan went off to college, we were keeping eight to nine horses here on this property. Dan was in charge of them. They were his responsibility. Glenn came to work for us about that time and was some help to Dan. Dan became an excellent rider, and during the next seven years Dan won more trophies than we could keep at our house. Two years in a row he won the National Championship in Quarter Horse Geldings with his great gelding, Peso Gold. These were just two of his many victories. He won ribbons and trophies in all events. He made Little Otoetta into a National Junior Quarter Horse champion. This meant that he had to win at Halter, at Western Pleasure, Reining, and other events. It was a great honor for him, and the whole family took pride in his accomplishments. Despite all his victories, he was always the same: friendly, courteous, and kind to friends and strangers. This boy has the heart of a champion.

Another part of the family story needs to be told. When Dan was a little boy, Mama Sue gave Dan a dog for Christmas, and Dan named his dog Bud. Bud was a Rhodesian Ridgeback without the ridge. But Bud was some kind of a dog. The rules about Bud were strong. Bud could not come in the house at all. Dan had to feed Bud, and only Dan had to feed him. And Dan had to wash Bud and clean up the yard after Bud. And Bud grew tall and Bud grew big, and Bud was not a house dog. But we learned after a year or so that after we went to bed at night, Dan would get up and let Bud in the house. And Bud would sleep at the end of Dan's bed.

But Bud had a problem. Bud smelled. Bud really had an odor problem. And Dan washed him and bathed him, regularly and religiously. But still that smell stayed with Bud. So Bud never came in our part of the house; Bud was never welcome there. But Dan fed Bud and Dan cared for Bud.

Occasionally, Bud would bite-as in the case of Mr. Shivers, Dan's principal. Or the case of Tommy Sims, a lawyer who worked for me. And once A. J. Foyt got treed in the game room, with Bud snapping at his rear end.

But Bud was a good dog. And then one day a bad thing happened. Dan went off to college at Tarleton and poor Bud was left at home. I left the office early that afternoon and supper was ready when I got home. Susie and I ate, in silence, and after hurriedly finishing supper, I told her I would feed Bud. Mama Sue said, "no," she had already fed Bud. I didn't ask *any* questions.

The next day I came home early again, and sure enough, I discovered that Mama Sue had already fed Bud. By the time the weather started getting cooler, I came home late one night and much to my surprise, sitting in the keeping room in front of a big fire, was Susie in a comfortable chair, with Bud softly snoring at her feet. Again, I remained silent.

JOE, SUSIE, HUNT, AND DAN

Several nights later it got colder, and I came home to find Bud sitting cozily in front of the fire. A week before Thanksgiving, Susie rearranged the furniture in our bedroom and found a place for Bud to sleep on a small sofa there with us. Bud had moved in to the big house.

How do you explain this? What caused the change? Well, the answer is easy, and this is the truth. Bud was important to Dan, and what was important to Dan was important to Mama Sue.

A P.S. about Bud. When Dan married Nancy Tribble and they moved to Brenham, Bud moved to Brenham with them. And to the day he died, Bud was Dan's closest friend.

God has blessed me in so many ways. But by far, the greatest blessing given to me has been my family. My wife and my two sons and now the families of my two sons, are my pride and joy. Despite the heartaches and sicknesses, the separations caused by World War II and the Korean War, we have all stood together. A man with a wife like mine and two great sons, regardless of all other circumstances, is the richest man in the world. I'm that man.

Lake George

Lake George has been very special to us, and I want to talk about it at this point in my memoirs.

One day in the middle '50s I met a very successful building contractor who owned a company called Gulf Construction. They were involved in a lawsuit with St. Joe Paper Company. My client Harley Walker became a friend of mine, and his wife Helen became a friend of Susie's. There were other lawsuits, but the Walkers were wonderful and talented people, and they became very important in our lives. It was in 1962 that they invited us to spend two weeks' vacation with them in the Adirondack Mountains of upper New York state on Lake George.

They told us of the wonderful, beautiful lake. They told us that this was where American history began, and they told us that the Lake George area was the greatest antique shopping area in America. And so we were introduced to Cape Cod Village, Hague on Lake George, New York. Those two weeks staying in the cottage called the Spinning Wheel, along a creek and a hundred yards from the lake, with evening trips to Vermont for dinners at wonderful restaurants, daytime visits to battlefields and Fort Ticonderoga, and a re-living of the American Revolution was about as good as it gets.

On rainy days we went to Vermont, and there were several rainy days. One day during this two-week period, on a very rainy day, the four of us went into the original Vermont Country Store in Weston. We wandered around this country store and met the owner, Vrest Orton, and his lovely wife. He turned out to be an extremely interesting man to us-a former writer for *The New York Times*, as well as the author of a number of books (*Vermont Afternoons with Robert Frost* and *The Forgotten Art of Building a Good Fireplace* are two). This was the beginning of another beautiful friendship. Those two weeks changed our lives.

The following summer, by chance, the American Bar Association had its annual meeting in Montreal, which just happens to be about 120 miles north of Ticonderoga (Lake George), New York. So after the three-day meeting in Montreal, Susie and I decided to drive by Cape Cod Village to see if they had a vacant cottage. We were lucky. Things were in a turmoil in this little compound of some 30 cottages, because the owner of the village had recently died. But we spent some 10 days enjoying the lake, meeting new friends, going to Vermont, having dinner with the Ortons, and experiencing a wonderful trip.

JOE, SUSIE, HUNT, AND DAN

Upon our return to Houston, we received word that the estate of the deceased owner was offering cottages for sale, and that those who had rented a cottage in '63 would be given first choice to buy a cottage. We were offered first chance at Sparrowhawk, a small cottage on the green, approximately a hundred yards from the lake. The selling price of this cottage was $10,000, and it needed a lot of repairs and certainly needed new furnishings. There was no way that we would ever make use of such a cottage, but before we left, we bought it!

For the next 30 or more years, Sparrowhawk became our home away from home. It's where we spent our summers. I became an authority on the American Revolution. Hunt and I went to Fort Ticonderoga every summer; we walked the battlefields at Saratoga, and we fought the sea battles on Lake Champlain, where the American Navy was born.

Susie spent her time buying antiques, especially old jugs with blue painting on them, which cost her $1 apiece. She acquired an interest in a china referred to as "Flow Blue," and lo and behold, I too became addicted to jugs and Flow Blue. Our house here in Houston is filled with both. Those simple antiques, which we bought for ridiculous prices, have today increased in value over a thousand percent.

But it was the lake, the beautiful Lake George, the most beautiful lake in the world to us, that attracted us the most. We loved Lake George. And still on those rainy days we would go to Vermont and we would have dinner at a great restaurant in Rutland, somewhere closer to Lake George. The Ortons became our very, very close friends.

I don't remember the year, but it had to be in the early '60s. We were having dinner with the Ortons at this wonderful restaurant in Rutland. And Mr. Orton, this wonderful man and friend, said,

"Joe, I am head of the Republican Party of Vermont. And you know we are a single-party state, because Democrats have not discovered us. And we have a vacancy in our Attorney General's office, and I have been authorized to offer you the appointment as Attorney General of Vermont if you and Susie will move here. And if you do, I can assure you that four years later, you will become Governor of Vermont."

But before I could even thank him for this wonderful honor, my beautiful, wonderful, pragmatic wife said "No way, José. We cannot ever leave Texas." This had to be Divine Provision or Divine Wisdom on her part, because several years later the hippies discovered Vermont, and they took over the state. Before that happened, though, Mr. Orton called me one day to tell me that his friend who owned the newspaper in Manchester, New Hampshire, had been sued for libel in federal court in New Hampshire for calling some liberal a dirty word. And Mr. Orton had prevailed upon his friend, the editor of the paper, to hire me as his lawyer. I did go and meet with the Manchester newspaper man and was able to get the case resolved by quick negotiations. But because of that experience, our friendship and love of Lake George doubled.

Our sweet granddaughter Jennifer (about whom you will hear more in the next chapter) usually spent every summer with us at Cape Cod Village, and she became addicted to Sparrowhawk, as did most of our family. But to Jennifer, it was paradise. And even in high school, she was able to work down at the Silver Bay YMCA Convention Center, just two miles from our cottage. The first summer she was making beds and being a maid, and her second summer she was a part of the concierge staff, where she worked with a boy by the name of John McEwan from California.

Later, Jennifer graduated from high school and became a student at Texas A&M, and she continued her visits to and work at Lake George. John McEwan transferred to Texas A&M, and lo and behold, a few years later, John and Jennifer got married. The marriage took place in the Charles Evans Hughes Chapel at Silver Bay Resort near our cottage in The Hague, on a very rainy night. Many of our friends from Houston came to that wedding, and it was a glorious, wonderful wedding. The reception was held in that beautiful hotel on Lake George, the Sagamore, where we ate and others danced. And to this day, except for my own, it's the most beautiful wedding I ever attended.

We continued to make our summer and especially fall trips to Sparrowhawk, but several years ago, I became extremely ill while there, and perhaps would have died, because there are no hospitals within 50 miles. But Mike Stevens sent his plane, picked us up, and flew me to Houston, where I was immediately taken to St. Luke's Hospital with a ruptured gall bladder. Believe it or not, I survived, but the doctors told me, "No more Lake George trips." So Jennifer and John took our place, and today they take their summer vacations and occasionally a fall trip to Cape Code Village, while Susie and I stay at home, enjoying our jugs and Flow Blue.

CHAPTER 5

The Grandchildren

Every grandparent, under the natural law as stated by Blackstone, has bragging rights. It is only by the exercise of considerable restraint that I limit my remarks about these four super, gifted, magnificent, fantastic grandchildren. I have to be extremely careful. To our grandchildren, and to our children, and to hundreds of others, Susie and I have become "Daddy Joe" and "Mama Sue."

JENNIFER

Jennifer was the first, and because of that, she has a special place in our hearts. But more than that, when Jennifer was born, she had difficulties, and as a result, Hunt, his wife Nancy (Darby), and Jennifer lived with us for the first three months of her life. At that time, I took the liberty of naming our home "Jennifer Park." My favorite time was to walk her to sleep and to sing to her where no one else could be critical of my singing. She thought I was Caruso. That was long ago. Now she knows better.

She has been a wonderful, wonderful granddaughter, and she has set a high standard for all the rest. She has fulfilled every dream and goal that we have had for her. She has added a dimension to our lives that we will never forget. Because of circumstances, she has been raised almost as if she were our daughter. Once when we were up at College Station, she took me by the hand and told me, "Daddy Joe, I want to marry a man just like you."

Jennifer, Mama Sue, and I have been like a circle. And the three of us have not only loved each other but we have been the closest of friends. She especially made us very proud when she graduated from Texas A&M University with a 4.0 GPA! She went on to get her master's and at this writing has completed all but her dissertation for her Ph.D. And now she is Mrs. John Campbell McEwan, and we are proud and happy to add John to our family. As of this writing, they have given us two great-grandchildren, William, who was born in February 2008, and Charles in October 2009.

As I mentioned before, Susie and I loved that cottage, Sparrowhawk, on Lake George in the Adirondacks near Fort Ticonderoga. We would rent it out during the summers, and then we would travel up there every fall to see the beautiful autumn leaves of New England. And Jennifer's meeting and marrying John was a capstone of our Lake George memories.

Clay

"Clay Boy" is next. He is a lot like his father Dan, and he is a boy who is quiet, but who loves deeply. His genuine affection for Dan and "Nancy-Dan" and Mama Sue and me is a tremendous tribute to us. I would trust this boy with my life. Today he has become a young man who continues to grow in stature and grace. He has become an expert in the raising and showing of cattle. There is not a lazy bone in his body, and he would do anything in the world to please us. He is truly a blessing. Clay's dedication to doing every job well reminds me of my own youth. Even though obstacles existed for me, and that I could never reach the goal I wanted, I gave it a bloody try. In all of this, I see Clay as I once lived.

THE GRANDCHILDREN

DANIELLE

Danielle is my sweetheart. She is very shy, but underneath her shyness, she is very sensitive and caring. She is a beautiful girl, and every day she becomes more so. She gets from her mother that wonderful trait of caring for people. If and when we can't get around, Nancy-Dan and Danielle will be there to take care of us. That I know. And that is one of the greatest assurances an older person can have. Danielle completed a two-year course of study in photography in Oklahoma, and she is now a professional photographer.

LISA

Lisa came into our lives when Hunt married Laura. She was six years old at the time, and we have enjoyed watching her grow into a young lady. She has now graduated from Texas A&M, and she and her husband Kent White, also an Aggie grad, are in the landscaping business and live in San Antonio. From her interest in photography to her love for her pets, Lisa excels. But it's more than that. Lisa is one of mine. She is a very special, beautiful girl of whom we are very proud. We love Lisa as we love the others. She is also very bright and gifted, but most of all, she is my friend.

We are grateful every day to have our lives blessed with these four grandchildren. Long after we are gone, they will continue our family legacy of honor, truth, good character, and love. Above all, they will know and teach their children, and their children's children, that love of the Lord is the most important thing in all of life, and with that truth in place in their lives, everything else will be all right.

Because this truth will always stand for all Believers: "For we *know* that all things work together for good to them that love the Lord; to them that are called according to His purpose." Romans 8:28.

Finally, if we have but one prayer for our grandchildren, it is that they will always read and apply and look to the Book of Proverbs for guidance. This book is the book of wisdom. "Trust in the Lord with all your heart and lean not on your own understanding. In all your ways acknowledge Him, and He shall direct your paths. Do not be wise in your own eyes. Fear the Lord and depart from evil. It will be health to your flesh and strength to your bones." Proverbs 3:5-8.

Mike and Kim

Mike and Kim Stevens have held very special places in our hearts. They were not our children, but many times we felt that they were. A great and painful sadness came into our lives when Michael Stevens succumbed to pneumonia after a battle with cancer in 2008 and went to be with our Lord. But I want to tell you about Mike.

The first day Hunt went to public schools in the first grade, he came home that afternoon and brought a boy by the name of Mike Stevens. When I came home from work that evening, Mike was there to eat supper with us. He was a wonderful little boy with a beautiful smile, and Mama Sue immediately fell in love with him.

After supper, Mike did not want to go home, but because the next day was a school day, we insisted that he go home, and finally around 8 o'clock, I took him down to his house two blocks away. I met his parents, both of whom had been drinking, and I then understood why Mike wanted to be at our house.

The next night when I came home from work, Mike was there, and so it happened for many, many weeks and months, even into years, that Mike became a part of our family. Mama Sue had become his security blanket, and she provided for Mike as she did for Hunt.

On the weekends Mike went to Sunday School and church with

THE GRANDCHILDREN

us, and Mike went on trips with us. When Hunt got a baseball bat, well, Mike got a bat. Or when Hunt got a glove, Mike got a glove. And when Hunt went to camp, Mike went to camp. Mike became a real part of our family, and we loved Mike with all our hearts. He was such a mischievous, yet gifted, young boy, and the years went by, and finally Mike graduated from high school.

Mike had been a great athlete, and he played on our little league team. He was a terrific pitcher. Of course, he and Hunt also did football and all the sports together in high school. But when Mike graduated from high school, he joined the Marine Corps.

The years went by, as they generally do, and we didn't see Mike, but we talked about him, we missed him, we wished for him, but we didn't know where or how he was. And then one day on an airplane, while Susie and I were flying to Denver to spend to weekend with our friends Bruce and Mary Ann Belin, I saw this young man with a beautiful girl, walking down the aisle of the plane. As they approached us, Mike leaned over and kissed Mama Sue and said, "Mama Sue, I'm Mike Stevens."

Later, after the plane was in the air, Susie and I walked back to where Mike and the girl were sitting, and Mike introduced us to his wife Kim, a wonderful, beautiful girl. Then Mike reached in his pocket and took out a little book, and there it was: "Things to Do." Number One on his list was "Call Mama Sue."

From that time on until the day he died, Mike and Kim came back in to our lives, and we were the better for it. They really and truly became part of our family. Mike was taken away from us way too soon, in 2008, after battling lymphoma and pneumonia. He will be missed so much by so many.

CHAPTER 6

Joe's Law Career Starts with a Bang

During Alan Shivers' tenure as Governor of Texas, Price Daniel (his Attorney General at the time) hired me as one of his assistants. General Daniel hired me because I was a war veteran. Just about everyone objected, because I was so young. But I went with him many places and even babysat his children, since I was not married. His comment to my detractors was, "Well, if he's old enough to fight at Iwo Jima, he's old enough to be on my staff."

How I landed this job is sort of interesting. My practice court professor at Baylor Law School was Judge Joe Hale. Since I was the "teacher's pet," he recommended me for one of the finest jobs available to any young lawyer in Texas. He had recommended me, and I had been accepted, as briefing attorney for Judge James P. Alexander, Chief Justice of the Supreme Court of Texas. This was one of the greatest opportunities a young lawyer could have. The only problem with the job was that the pay was $75 a month.

Notwithstanding all of this, my cousin-in-law Joe Greenhill, was leaving the same position. (Joe's wife Martha is my first cousin; her mother and Beppie were sisters.) Joe had been selected by Attorney General Price Daniel to be head of the trial and appellate division of the Texas Attorney General's office. That section represented the State of Texas in all of its lawsuits, and there were about 20 lawyers in the section. They tried cases all over Texas.

After Joe had learned that I was going to work for the Supreme Court, he called and said that Attorney General Daniel had authorized Joe to hire me to work in the AG's office, at a much higher salary, and Joe strongly recommended that I take the job with the AG, because it afforded me the opportunity to try jury cases all over Texas, and that he would make me into "first-class trial lawyer."

Shortly thereafter, I received a special telegram from Attorney General Daniel, advising me that I had passed the bar exam and was to report to work on April 21, 1947. [!] So it was with the proverbial fear and trepidation that I called Mr. Chief Justice Alexander to tell him that I was going to work for the AG's office in the trial division. He expressed his sincere opinion that my opportunity to work in the trial section of the AG's office was "as good as it gets." And he strongly recommended that I take the job. Even Judge Hale thought it was the opportunity of a lifetime.

So it was that I arrived in Austin, the capital of Texas, on that Monday morning, April 21, walked to the capitol, and found it locked! After knocking on the door of the capitol, a Texas Ranger came to the door and explained to me that the capitol was closed, because it was a Texas holiday. This was San Jacinto Day, celebrated throughout Texas as the day Texas gained its freedom from Mexico as a result of that short, decisive, all-important battle back in 1836, led by Sam Houston against Santa Anna. This was the defeat of Mexico that allowed Texas to become a republic. In my anxious state about beginning this new job, I had completely forgotten the importance of that date!

But I had my orders, and being a good soldier, I persisted and eventually found an open door. I then made my way to the Attorney

JOE'S LAW CAREER STARTS WITH A BANG

General's library, where I walked into a sitting room filled with books. There was one man, all alone, surrounded by books. This man was to have an important effect on and be a major part of my life. It was Joe Greenhill.

He said, "Am I glad to see you! I'm preparing for a deposition in the *Sweatt* case this Saturday, and I have to make a talk Friday at noon at the St. David's Episcopal Church on *The Trial of Christ*. Would you prepare me some notes for that talk at St. David's?"

My first day as a lawyer was spent studying the trial of Christ. You can't beat that for beginning a law career.

While Price Daniel was my ultimate boss, Joe Greenhill was my immediate boss. Joe Greenhill was and is the greatest appellate lawyer in Texas. He gave me lawsuit assignments, and I tried them, every week, and they were mostly jury trials. You couldn't do that today. Back then, most cases took three days to try. A long case took a week. Depositions were almost unheard of.

That *Sweatt* case Joe Greenhill was working on that San Jacinto Day I reported for duty was a very famous case called *Sweatt v. Painter*, and Joe was the lawyer in charge. It was a civil rights case involving Heman Sweatt, the first black who applied to the University of Texas School of Law. As my first official duty as a lawyer, Joe assigned me to take a deposition in Prairie View, Texas, in that case. I had never been to a deposition. But I prepared and went to Prairie View, and the lawyer on the other side was a man named Thurgood Marshall, who treated me as if I knew what I was doing. He treated me as an equal. He, of course, later took a seat on the United States Supreme Court. I'd say my beginning as a lawyer was auspicious, to say the least.

While in the AG's office, I was assigned to try state antitrust cases, but primarily I represented the Highway Department in all types of litigation. It was a busy two-year period.

Joe Greenhill was my great, great mentor. More than anything else, I learned about demeanor. I learned to respect courts and judges. I learned that "Rambo" doesn't work in the courtroom, and I learned that collegiality is the only way to practice law.

In the fall of 2008, I was featured in *The Houston Lawyer* magazine's "A Profile in Professionalism." I submitted an article about my personal rules for achieving success, which are:

- Rule 1: Let your word be your bond.
- Rule 2: The lawyer on the other side is neither your enemy nor your client's enemy. He or she is a lawyer doing a job.
- Rule 3: Delaying tactics, especially in the discovery process, never aid your cause of justice but cause courts and juries to question your motives.
- Rule 4: Let bringing justice and enjoying the courtroom be your goals.

Let me repeat: the lawyer on the other side is not your enemy. He- or nowadays she-is a professional doing what you're doing. But the most important rule is Rule 1: Let your word be your bond. Since that article was published, I have received many calls, letters, and e-mail messages complimenting me on these rules for success. Even lawyers that I don't know have been gracious in telling me that they have adopted these rules for themselves.

In the last few years I have served as a mediator in many cases, and in a few of them I was a friend of the lawyers on both sides. I told them, "We're not going to have any arguing and fighting and name-calling, because I won't put up with that. It's not necessary, and it makes you look bad. It makes our profession look bad." They didn't like it, but they did it.

Things were collegial when I started practicing law. The Thurgood Marshall example is a case in point. I was just a kid that day, who

JOE'S LAW CAREER STARTS WITH A BANG

knew nothing. Mr. Marshall was a very experienced lawyer, one of the great lawyers of America, and he treated me as an equal professionally. He was courteous. He was kind. He was helpful. He wasn't trying *me*; he just wanted the facts. And that's what Joe Greenhill taught me. Later on in my career, I became Chairman of the Board of Visitors of the Thurgood Marshall School of Law at Texas Southern University, and I was very proud to serve.

During my two and a half years in the AG's office, I went all over Texas trying lawsuits, and I probably tried more lawsuits to juries than most lawyers will try in a lifetime.

After those fabulous years in the Texas Attorney General's office, working with Joe Greenhill as my immediate boss, I took a job in Houston with a small but excellent law firm, Bracewell & Tunks. Mr. J. S. (Searcy) Bracewell was a great man and a great lawyer, and Bert Tunks, considered by many people to be the best lawyer they've ever seen, was my immediate boss. He was a trial lawyer; he was a quiet man; he was a brilliant man. He took me with him, and I carried his briefcase.

These two men, together with Joe Greenhill in the AG's office, gave me the fantastic opportunity of being mentored by the greatest of lawyers. But there was a third lawyer who mentored me. That man was Colonel Leon Jaworski. My relationship with him was primarily because I had gone to Baylor. He took me under his wing and was like a father to me. He was responsible for my induction into the American College of Trial Lawyers, an organization of which I am proud to be a part.

In reality, Colonel Jaworski practically invented depositions in Texas, and that was during the famous *Billy Sol Estes* case. I was on a plane with Colonel Jaworski while that case was going on, and he was sending an associate to California to take about a hundred depositions. The colonel told me: "Let me tell you something, young man. Every time you go into that courtroom, I want you to know what every witness is going to say before he gets on the stand. And the only way you can do that is by deposition."

I said, "My clients can't afford depositions, Colonel." And he said, "Well, then they ought not get into a lawsuit." And that's the way it started.

In the early 1950s, Will Wilson, who was then Attorney General of Texas, asked me to represent the state of Texas in an antitrust suit against all of the electrical contractors in Texas. I was a private lawyer at the time, but I agreed to accept the assignment. The lawyers on the other side included some greats: Colonel Leon Jaworski, Jack Binion, Leroy Jeffers, Tom Martin Davis, Tom Phillips Sr., and Ben Sewell. They were the among the greatest lawyers in Texas, and I was the little whippersnapper on the other side. Again, those men treated me as an equal. As things turned out, I won that case, against all of those giants, and it was quite an experience.

My first case to try in Houston was in Judge Holland's court, *Schilling v. City of Houston*. That case involved Mrs. Schilling, who was seriously injured by a city garbage truck, but under the doctrine of "The King Can Do No Wrong," the city had no liability for operating a garbage truck. But Mr. Bracewell conjured up the idea of suing the city for operating a garage that failed to properly repair the brakes on the garbage truck. My recollection is that the jury gave me a verdict of about $80,000, which at that time was one of the biggest verdicts in Harris County. Things have changed.

It would be tempting to go into numerous cases from those days, but it might border on cruel and unusual punishment to make you sit through all these trials. Perhaps on a rainy day, or when insomnia strikes, that will be the topic for another book, or at least an appendix to this history. I prefer to hit the high spots.

JOE'S LAW CAREER STARTS WITH A BANG

One interesting story I'm reminded of when I think about the importance of Iwo Jima is also tied to our house on Lynbrook. After my hospitalization from my wounds at the Battle of Iwo Jima, I had been sent back to Guam and assigned the task of a criminal investigator of Japanese war crimes. So I had a relief map of the island of Iwo Jima, and I managed to make it back to Houston with that map. Susie's dad had that map mounted on a huge 4' x 6' piece of plywood, and it hung on a wall in the original house on Stamper Way, which we had bought from Susie's parents.

When we bought the house on Lynbrook, Susie said that thing was not going to be hung, and it didn't match any of her decor. And she was right. So it found a place of neglect in the attic. When we moved from that house to our present house on Memorial Drive, we totally forgot about that Iwo Jima relief map Mr. Stamper had taken such pains to mount for display.

A few years after we had moved, I was contacted by someone in the State Department or at the Pentagon (can't remember which) who said that they were glad to have finally tracked down that relief map and would I mind giving it to them. But it wasn't exactly a question. However, they did offer that I could have a $100,000 credit against future income taxes to use as I chose. Think about it: a $100,000 tax credit!

Susie called the owners of the Lynbrook house and asked if that mounted relief map of Iwo Jima might still be there in the attic at 6226 Lynbrook. The answer was: "Oh, do you mean that rubber thing that was all melted on a piece of plywood?" Uh-oh. Goodbye tax credit. Attics in Houston summers can reach the 120s or the 130s-Farenheit. Not exactly a "high spot" of my career, but a story worth telling, don't you think?

But how about this story about a suit where I represented Nolan Bush, a brakeman, against the MK&T ("Katy") Railroad in

LaGrange, Fayette County, Texas, home of the infamous "Chicken Ranch." My client, Mr. Bush, was riding in the caboose and some black teenage boys threw rocks through the open caboose window, hitting Mr. Bush's left eye and putting it out.

The judge was Judge Williams, and Dan Moody, who had been a very famous governor of Texas, represented the railroad. Dan Moody was recognized as the leading trial lawyer in Texas, and even the judge was enamored of him. It was pretty obvious.

A man on the jury panel, who ran a filling station in Bastrop, Texas, had one eye. I didn't strike him, because I was sure Gov. Moody would. But he didn't! Apparently he thought the juror would de-emphasize the value of losing one eye, feeling that it wasn't worth much money.

During the trial my co-counsel, LaGrange lawyer Joe Hart, a Marine buddy, was trying to get some photos into evidence. There are certain hoops to jump through in order to get photos admitted into evidence in a trial. Joe didn't do it right, and every time he tried to get one in, Gov. Moody would object, and the judge would sustain it. I went up to Joe and whispered in Joe's ear the words he should use to get the photos admitted. With that, Gov. Moody jumped up and said, "Your Honor, I object to Mr. Reynolds coaching his co-counsel."

Judge Williams pointed his finger at me and said, "You son of a bitch! You sit down and shut up!"

I told the judge I took deep exception to his remarks and that they were totally out of order and had no place in the courtroom. I asked the court reporter if she "got all that down." I then added to Judge Williams that I moved for a mistrial, and I further told him, "Judge I will be compelled to file a complaint against you with the Supreme Court of Texas." It just so happened at the time one

JOE'S LAW CAREER STARTS WITH A BANG

of the Justices of the Supreme Court was my Evidence professor, Judge Abner McCall, who had offered me a job in his law firm in Corsicana upon my graduation from law school.

A woman spectator on the front row of the courtroom jumped up and said, "Judge Williams, I demand an apology from you to every woman in this courtroom, and I want it now." He sat there for a while, and she said, "I'm waiting, Judge. And if you don't apologize now, my husband will come in and whip you." About that time, the sheriff walked in, and the lady said, "Judge, I believe you know my husband."

Judge Williams said, "Mr. Reynolds, forgive me. I apologize. And Ladies and Gentlemen of the jury, I've done a bad thing. I'm sorry," or words to that effect.

The jury awarded my client $80,000 in damages, which in those days was astronomical. And the one-eyed man from Bastrop was the foreman of the jury.

I went through with filing the complaint with the Supreme Court. I just had to do it. When it landed on Judge McCall's desk, the first call I got was from Judge McCall, and the second call was from Judge Williams.

About six months later, I was in court in Brenham, and Judge Williams walked in. At that time, the judges "rode a circuit" that covered about six counties. When he saw me, he smiled, and from that point on, you would have thought I was his best friend.

But that story's not over yet. Gov. Moody failed to file a supersedeas bond, and I immediately had Sheriff Fluornoy levy a writ of execution upon the Katy Railroad. We commandeered and took possession of a Katy Railroad steam engine as it was passing through LaGrange, Texas. I got an emergency call from

Gov. Moody, and it was not a friendly call. He was very disturbed that anybody would be so gross as to levy execution against the Katy Railroad. I merely followed the law.

I don't remember, and I'm not sure there's anybody left alive who would know, but I think we settled that case soon after that phone call.

That case is reported at 310 S.W.2d 404 (Tex. Civ. App. —Austin 1958), *Missouri-Kansas-Texas Railroad Co. v. Nolan Lee Bush*.

I was reminded of this story when my great friend and a great Houston lawyer named Diana Marshall called me in November 2008 to ask me to co-chair a trial in Fayette County, because someone had recommended me, since I had tried so many cases there. It reminded me of this and many other memories of cases in that special part of Texas, but sadly, at age 87, Susie would not be pleased with my accepting such an assignment. She would tell me to get to work on my book.

But, before we can hit any more of the high spots, I have to note that, despite starting my legal career with a bang, that career soon took a nosedive. I was called back into the Marine Corps.

CHAPTER 7

Joe's "Adventures" in Korea

The battle of Chosin Reservoir has been called one of the bloodiest battles in Marine Corps history (another is Iwo Jima). That famous battle began about November 26, 1950, in the mountains of North Korea, in an area known as Jang Jin Ho. Some historians have described it as the most savage battle in modern warfare. President Reagan mentioned it in his first inaugural address as one of the epics of military history.

On November 26 the campaign began at Yudam-ni as the Chinese Communists attacked the 5th and 7th Marine Regiments on the west side of the reservoir. By November 28, the battle spread throughout the 1st Marine Division section of the area.

About 20,000 troops (17,000 of whom were from the 1st Marine Division) along with the 7th Infantry Division and the 41 Independent Commando from the U.K. were attacked by 120,000 Chinese Communists whose orders were to annihilate the allies "to the last man." That bloody battle, although relatively unknown to many Americans today, is unparalleled in modern history. As I remember the figures, of our 15,000 allied casualties, 2,500 were killed in action, 5,000 were wounded in action, and 7,500 suffered severe frostbite and cold injuries. Our enemy did not fare as well, with 40,000 dead and thousands more wounded.

In August 1950, I was a Very Busy Man. I had become a lawyer. I had a job with the prestigious law firm of Bracewell & Tunks. I was on my way-so I thought. Each morning I read The *Houston Post* to see if the Philadelphia Phillies might really win the National League pennant, and I worried and wondered about the coming football season.

On the morning of August 12, I arrived at the office as usual, read the paper, and then started on the mail. One letter looked very official. I opened it last. Finally, as I cautiously opened this last letter, I read, "Greetings-you have been called back into active duty in the United States Marine Corps. Ten days from this date you will report for active duty at Camp Pendleton, Oceanside, California."

They couldn't do that to me! I was married. I had a year-old son. I was a lawyer. I was a Texan. I had a case up for trial before 127th District Court Judge William M. Holland in two weeks. I couldn't go.

By the middle of the afternoon I had grown accustomed to the idea, and I approached my sweet wife with bravado. I entered the house as if I had won a great prize. I explained the letter, and I drew my wife a picture of Laguna Beach, California. It would be a vacation at government expense. She and Hunt, our one-year-old son, would love it. I would be a legal officer at Camp Pendleton; we'd have a ball.

I caught the train at the old Southern Pacific Station and arrived at Camp Pendleton on a Sunday night. Two days later I went aboard ship and, three weeks from the day I left Houston, I stormed ashore at the battle of Inchon, Korea.

JOE'S "ADVENTURES" IN KOREA

I was still a lawyer, I was still a Texan, and they still couldn't do this to me. But there I was.

Inchon is not far from the large city of Seoul, but we had to fight the North Koreans for every inch of ground to reach Seoul. To get there we had to attack and capture the Kimpo air strip and, finally, we encircled the city before its capture.

I was one of the first Marines to cross the Han River in the attack on Seoul.

Maybe it was me. Maybe it was the circumstances. But I didn't like Korea. I found it dirty and dusty, and I didn't like being shot at. Besides, the Korean people were fickle. Some of them liked us, and some of them didn't. And North Koreans looked just like South Koreans.

The First Marine Division, of which I was a part, finally took Seoul. Eventually, we reached the 38th parallel. On the way, we had many casualties, and we took many North Korean prisoners. It was a relatively easy campaign compared to Iwo Jima, but I was glad to reach the 38th parallel. We thought the war was over.

I was ready to go home, but that was not to be. We were transported back to Inchon in trucks, then loaded aboard old Japanese LSTs, and then we sailed around the South Korean horn and proceeded north through the minefields of the Japanese Sea. We made an amphibious landing in the North Korean port of Wonsan.

A word about those Japanese LSTs. They were *bad*. They were dirty, and in a matter of days we, too, smelled. By now, it was October. The weather was changing. Sleeping in foxholes was no fun.

Word came down that our objective was to reach the Yalu River, the boundary between North Korea and China. We were told that on the way we were to capture the power plant at the south end of the Chosin Reservoir. Our approach march was up a narrow valley, surrounded by high, snow-covered mountains, and our objective, the Yalu River, was about 100 miles to the north.

The mountains were tough, but the opposition was light, and we pushed up.

I remember November 11 especially. We were still wearing our light clothing. That night, a norther blew in. The next morning it was 11 degrees Fahrenheit. It got colder. In two weeks, the temperature was 40 below zero. We were issued parkas, gloves, and shoe packs (which did little more than filter the wind). Moreover, we still had to sleep on the ground-and sleep was impossible.

Later (*much* later), when I got home, J. S. Bracewell asked me how cold it was. I asked him if he had ever been in a frozen food locker. When he said yes, I suggested if he would go into a frozen food locker in his underwear and stay a month, he would have a pretty good idea as to how cold it really was. It was so cold that you could literally grasp your breath. If you placed a metal spoon or fork on your mouth, the spoon or fork would freeze to your lips. Removing the spoon or fork from your lips was a major operation. And it got colder-and colder. There were no fires, no warmth. Just cold.

Then came Thanksgiving. That night, we had very little to be thankful for. The Chinese Communists, around midnight, crossed the Yalu River into North Korea and entered the Korean War.

Our outfit was on the western side of the Chosin Reservoir, several miles from the Yalu. The Marines at the reservoir numbered approximately 12,000. We were hit by more than 100,000 Chinese soldiers.

JOE'S "ADVENTURES" IN KOREA

The Chinese came into the war at my position. As stated, they hit about midnight, and we were in a fight for our lives. At the first onslaught, we fell back to our second position, approximately 200 yards to the rear. We set up a crisscrossing line of rifle fire. We killed Chinese by the hundreds. Those we didn't kill stopped, looted, and fought each other over the gear we had left in the first foxholes.

When daylight came, our fighter planes strafed and continued to strafe the Chinese. We were able to hold our position. By noon, however, we learned that we were totally surrounded. It was at this time that Major General Oliver P. Smith, our commanding officer, issued his famous statement: "Retreat, hell. We'll just attack in another direction."

We formed a perimeter, a circle, sort of like the pioneers of old who would circle their wagons to fight the Indians. We fought the Chinese from every direction. We moved like a rubber band, always moving to the south. We would stretch and pull up and stretch and pull up. For the next three weeks, we fought in this manner, trying to fight our way through the Chinese encirclement.

Foot problems were one of my legacies from Korea, and although the frostbite was fierce, my foot damage turned out to be made much worse from losing the arches in my feet. During one of the Korean battles, I was standing on an embankment, and a land mine exploded somewhere nearby. This caused the embankment I was standing on to collapse, and I fell down about 15 or 20 feet. Thankfully, I landed in a pile of snow, which saved my life, but my feet were messed up for the rest of my life.

Another night, just below the little North Korean town of Koto-Ri, we ran into serious trouble. My outfit had the east flank. A young man by the name of Francis Mintor (who had entered the war straight from Milby High School) was our point corporal. He led our outfit along a railroad embankment. It was pitch dark. Sometime around midnight, Mintor called for me, and I came running. He told me there was a horde of Chinese on the other side of the embankment, and that they were about to attack.

As the Chinese came over the embankment, Mintor squeezed the trigger of his Browning Automatic Rifle, and I squeezed the trigger of my M-1 carbine. Neither the BAR or the carbine fired. Both firing pin of the BAR and the firing pin of my carbine were frozen. It saved our lives. Some 20 Chinese came over the embankment and surrendered to us. This is the only time I was ever grateful for the cold.

Somewhere along the push south, I was wounded in both feet by a Chinese mortar shell. Because of the cold, I felt no pain. For over a hundred miles and nearly two weeks, I walked on seriously injured feet. By the time we reached safety at Hung Nam, several weeks later, both feet were the size of footballs.

I was evacuated to a hospital in Japan and spent approximately a year recovering.

Korea was an interesting country, and I remember very clearly when we went through the city of Hung Nam, North Korea, on Halloween night, 1950. The Korean people were standing on the streets waving their United Nations flags and calling us heroes. I also remember several weeks later, when we were retreating back to Hung Nam, that these same people were standing on those same street corners, this time waving communist flags and throwing sticks and stones at us.

Korea has changed a great deal since 1950. During the Korean War, we found that things were primitive. For the most part, women were beasts of burden. Men carried rice in wooden pallets on their heads and women washed clothes. beating them with rocks.

JOE'S "ADVENTURES" IN KOREA

Today, Korea is an industrialized country. Since 1950, Christianity has made a tremendous impact on Korea. They tell me that the moral fiber of the people has undergone a tremendous change, for the better. It is hard to relate or compare today's Korea to the Korea as I knew it in 1950.

Several years ago, the Marine Corps sponsored the creation of an organization called The Chosin Few. We were given a citation, which read as follows: "Whatever we were in that frozen long ago and whatever we are now, we are bound as one for life in an exclusive fraternity of honor. The only way into our ranks is to have paid the dues of duty, sacrifice and valor by being there. The cost of joining is short and is beyond all earthly wealth."

Suffice it to say, if the Olympics were to be again held in Korea, I would prefer to be at home watching on television.

I believe it was Thanksgiving of 1991 when Hunt, Mike, Dan, and I were driving to College Station to see the annual Thanksgiving game between Texas A&M and Texas. While driving, Mike asked me what was my most memorable Thanksgiving. I said, "give me a few minutes."

Perhaps an hour later, as we approached College Station, I was ready to answer the question. They couldn't even remember the question. Nevertheless, I answered it. It's a true story, and this poem resulted from that question and my answer about my most memorable Thanksgiving.

KOREA 1950

One bitter night near Koto-ri,
I captured one of the enemy.
He read my eyes and knew the deal-
He knew at once I had to kill.

TOUCHED BY GRACE

>In broken English, he made request
>To see the picture in his vest.
>I nodded "Yes" above battle noise,
>And stared with him at wife and boys.
>
>"Go!" I screamed. "Get out of here!"
>He turned and ran and disappeared.
>Oft I've wondered if he made it home-
>Or is he buried in Korea's loam?
>
>Did he ever again his family see?
>But I've wondered most,
>Were roles reversed,
>How he would have treated me.
>
>*-Joe H. Reynolds*
>*-Captain, USMC*
>*Written in November 1991*

When I returned from Korea, I was interviewed many times, but an article I wrote for Lynn Ashby and *The Houston Post* pretty well explains what happened to me in Korea. After so many tears freezing on our faces and our long "fight in another direction," the straggling, struggling First Marine Division finally reached safety at the port city of Hung Nam in North Korea. This was the same city where we had been welcomed as heroes as we began our long march to the Chosin Reservoir.

I arrived at that spot in a terrible physical condition. As I said before, my feet were the size of footballs, and I was suffering from severe frostbite, but it was the same frostbite that allowed me to walk on those busted-up feet without pain. As my feet began to thaw, the pain became intense, and I was evacuated, along with many others, to a hospital in Japan. I was first carried to a U.S. Army hospital in Fuka Yoka at the southern tip of the Japanese Islands.

JOE'S "ADVENTURES" IN KOREA

The first thing they did to me was to cut off my clothes, which I had been wearing continually for months. I was then thrown into a hot shower, where I came alive again after those many weeks of freezing. Several days later, I was transferred to the naval hospital and port at Yakuska, Japan. Of the 15,000 Marines at the Chosin, 6,000 of us were in that hospital. I was put in a large room with blankets on the floor to serve as my bed, with an adjoining room the size of a closet, occupied by a friend of mine, Captain Bill Barber.

Through happenstance, I was placed in the smaller room with Bill, where the two of us lay on the floor recuperating from our wounds. Bill had been shot through the hip and was unable to walk. I could move on my knees and crawl, but I could not walk. Fortunately for all of us, a young naval lieutenant JG by the name of Bob Shoen, from Houston, Texas, whose wife Jane was one of Susie's high school friends, was recuperating from pneumonia in that very hospital. Bob took it upon himself to see that the 30 or so men in these two rooms were properly fed. There were insufficient hospital personnel to care for this number of wounded. Bob Schoen was a miracle.

Unknown to me, while I lay in that room, Bob discovered a Japanese short-wave radio operator and coerced this Jap to send a message to a ham operator in Bellaire, Texas, asking him to call Susie's daddy at Humble Oil, to tell him that I was alive and well. That afternoon in Houston, Daddy Bo rushed home and told Susie and Hunt that Daddy Joe was alive. They had not heard from me in weeks, and all they knew was that the First Marine Division had been surrounded by a Chinese horde at the Chosin Reservoir. Through these days at Yakuska, Bill Barber and I became like brothers. When he was able to walk, he and I both were reassigned to another hospital, this time at Otsu, Japan, and after that to another Army hospital in Kyoto, Japan, then back to Otsu. During all these hospital transfers, the doctors and nurses were pumping drugs into me to stimulate the circulation.

◄ TOUCHED BY GRACE

When back at Otsu, one morning they rushed in and told me that there was a passenger ship that was leaving Japan in several days, and that I had been selected to be sent home aboard that ship. On the morning of departure, my friend Bill Barber arranged somehow for a Jeep, and he drove me to the port of debarkation. While waiting to go aboard ship, I stood there in the only clothes I owned, freezing to death. My friend Barber took off his bloody, bullet-torn parka and threw it across my shoulders as he said, "Here is a Christmas present for you."

After these interesting tours of three different hospitals, where I was exposed to some unconventional therapies, I was finally sent to the naval hospital at Corpus Christi, Texas. In December of 1951 I was given the option of an additional six months in another medical hospital, in North Carolina, or resign my Marine Corps commission and give up my medical disability benefits. I chose the latter and gave up those benefits, so that I could go back and become a lawyer once again.

Fifty years later, Bill Barber came back into my life. Susie and I went to Newport Beach, California, knowing that Bill lived there. We called him and told him we would be there, and on arrival at the John Wayne Airport, Susie made a present to Bill of his still bloodstained, bullet-pierced parka. (It still fit.)

Incidentally, Bill was awarded the Medal of Honor for his heroic role of leading Fox Company at the Chosin. When Mike Stevens went through the Marine Corps and was taught Military Tactics, the prime example used in instructing present-day Marines was Fox Company, Seventh Marines, led by Bill Barber at the Chosin Reservoir. The stories are endless, but there's an old saying: "Once a Marine, always a Marine."

In 1952 America was involved in a Presidential election. Much to my surprise, Governor Shivers, heading up Democrats for Eisenhower,

JOE'S "ADVENTURES" IN KOREA

asked if I would speak, for Eisenhower. I did, and it was a great experience. The night before the election, I was on national TV for approximately 30 minutes.

Here is an unsolicited letter I received from General Eisenhower, the original of which hangs in my office, proudly framed:

OFFICE OF DWIGHT D. EISENHOWER

Hotel Commodore
New York 17, New York
December 16, 1952

Dear Joe:

The deep admiration and regard which I feel for all veterans is enhanced in your case by a sense of special gratitude for the work you did in our campaign. I was honored to have your support and assistance.

With best wishes,

Sincerely,

/s/ Dwight D. Eisenhower

Mr. Joe Reynolds
San Jacinto Building
Houston, Texas

I was and still am very proud of that letter. I am also proud of a commendation I received for service in Korea, but I want to publicly say that this commendation should be awarded to everybody who served there. Here is the letter that was presented with the medal:

UNITED STATES MARINE CORPS
HEADQUARTERS
1ST MARINE DIVISION (REINF) FMF
c/o FLEET POST OFFICE
SAN FRANCISCO, CALIFORNIA

The Commanding General, 1st Marine Division (Reinf) FMF, takes pleasure in commending
FIRST LIEUTENANT JOE H. REYNOLDS
UNITED STATES MARINE CORPS RESERVE

for service as set forth in the following CITATION:

"For excellent service in the line of his profession while serving with a Marine artillery battalion during operations in KOREA from 2 November to 10 December 1950. First Lieutenant REYNOLDS, serving as an assistant operations officer in an artillery battalion, displayed great skill, courage, and confidence in the performance of his duties. Throughout this period he worked long tedious hours under adverse weather conditions, supervising and directing the efficient operations of an artillery fire direction team. During the movement of the division from Yudam-ni, Korea, to Chinhung-ni, Korea, he constantly exposed himself to accurate enemy small arms, mortar, and machine gun fire in order to direct the fire of his battalion on numerous enemy emplacements and road blocks along the way. His timely actions and complete disregard for his own personal safety were directly instrumental in the successful movement of the division, thereby setting an example for all who served with him and materially contributing to the success achieved by his battalion. First Lieutenant REYNOLDS' conduct throughout was in keeping with the highest traditions of the United States Naval Service."

Commendation Ribbon with Combat "V" Authorized.
/s/ G. C. Thomas

G. C. THOMAS,
Major General
U.S. Marine Corps

My Marine Corps story has many other unwritten chapters that have been told by me to family and friends. I conclude this chapter with a report that in 2000, I received a beautiful portrait of the Marine Corps Memorial in Washington, D.C. This beautiful picture, which now graces my new library in our home, is inscribed as follows:

"To Joe Reynolds
Thanks for your service and leadership"
Semper Fideles

/s/ C. C. Krulak
Commandant of the Marine Corps

It constantly reminds me of a great story I want to share. Sometime around 1998 I had a unique experience. I had lunch with the then Commandant of the Marine Corps in Houston, when General Krulak came for a meeting of the Board of Directors of Conoco Oil Company, on which he served. Archie Dunham, Conoco's president and a friend of mine from Second Baptist Church, had set up the luncheon.

When I arrived at Archie's office on the 20th floor, I was ushered to a large reception room, and Archie's secretary greeted me and said, "Follow me. You've having lunch in Mr. Dunham's private dining room." I had never laid eyes on General Krulak, who had just retired from the Marines. When I arrived for our private luncheon, he got up, came over to me, put his arms around my neck, said "I'm Chuck Krulak, Commandant of the Marine Corps." All I could say was "Wow." He then told me how much he admired and respected me. He said that I, Joe Reynolds, had been personally involved in the two greatest battles in Marine Corps history, and he wanted to meet one of the few men alive today who could make that claim.

During the luncheon, General Krulak said to me, "Tell me about the poem. It's a true story, isn't it?" And of course he knew it was. But more memorable to me was that in the course of this memorable three-hour visit, General Krulak told me of his fabulous experience in Desert Storm. He was the commanding general of the Third Marine Division and General Schwartzkopf gave him the responsibility of driving the Iraqis out of Kuwait. General Krulak was given a time of departure to start the battle, and he explained that it was impossible, because the Third Marine Division had run out of water. General Krulak had estimated that for his division to carry out its mission, a minimum of a million gallons of water would be needed. They had none.

General Krulak then told me an amazing and unbelievable story about how they came upon some kind of an oasis that had not been there before, and from that oasis they got the water they needed to complete their mission. He had me in the palm of his hand with this great story-one I was blessed to have heard from the horse's mouth.

As I was leaving that day, General Krulak put his arms around my shoulders and asked me, "Joe, do you know what one Marine says to another Marine when he's fixing to make a landing on a foreign shore?" I said, "Yessir." And he said, "Say it to me." And I said, "General, I'll see you on the beach."

He gripped my hand hard, and said to me, "I'll make you a promise. You're a lot older than I am, and you'll probably get there before I do, but I'll see you on the beach." In my later years, that saying has become one of my favorites.

Like all Marines, I gripe and complain about some of the things that happened to me during my time in the Marines, but I wouldn't

JOE'S "ADVENTURES" IN KOREA

change it for the world. I loved the Marine Corps, and I still do. My friends of old are still my friends, and the truth of the matter is that my time in the Marines molded my life and gave me foundations and teachings and experiences that have had a tremendous impact.

I would like to sum up what I think is my song for America, the land that I love. I believe with all my heart that every American boy who wears an American military uniform is an American hero. My other strong belief is that no President should ever have the right to send American troops into a war that America does not intend to win.

The Marine Corps is a big part of my life. I loved it. It shaped me into what I am and gave me experiences that not only led me to a deeper walk with the Lord Jesus Christ but gave me experiences that would take me through every hardship, problem, defeat, and disappointment our family has ever had. But most of all, my service as a Marine taught me that there was a fellowship, a family big and small, that is more important than life.

Fast-forwarding to Houston 1996, I was asked to speak and deliver a prayer at the annual Christmas gathering of Houston cadets of the U. S. Military Academy and the Midshipmen of the U. S. Naval Academy. I have been asked by several people for a copy of that prayer, so I have included it here:

Our Father, Who art in Heaven,

Tonight as we look upon this circle of youth, may each of their hearts have a longing to perpetuate the American Dream. The American Dream built upon the twin pillars of religious freedom for all men and equal opportunity for all men.

Make us aware that all good things come from Thee, and Thou dost give to each of us the responsibility of preserving them.

◄ TOUCHED BY GRACE

Impress upon our selfishness that we are not owners but stewards.

Sanctify our love of country that we might love America, take pride in America, and pass it on to our children and our children's children as the land of the free and the home of the brave.

Help us to make this God's own country by living like God's own people.

Through the strong, mighty name of Jesus Christ,

Amen

CHAPTER 8

Back To Joe's Law Career and Houston I.S.D.

Now that I was out of uniform, I returned to Bracewell & Tunks to pursue my dream of being a young Perry Mason. This is not a good description, because Bert Tunks and Mr. Bracewell made me into a civil litigator, and I didn't practice criminal law with that firm. But in those times, Perry Mason was a very famous "lawyer" and remained so for many years in books and on TV.

Shortly after I returned from Korea, a writer named Kaplan for *The Houston Press* wrote a huge article about me, stating in effect that I was a great hero of the Korean War. But like the news media of today, his story was full of exaggeration. Notwithstanding the exaggeration, the notoriety I received was amazing.

One of the persons who read this stuff was a man named Max Adloff, and he called me for lunch, and thus began beautiful friendship. Max decided that I had a message to give to Houston and Texas, so he took it upon himself to schedule me to speak to every service club-Rotary, Kiwanis, Exchange, and others-and lo and behold, I found myself making speeches all over Texas. I did that speech so many times, that it became a work of memory. Max Adloff would always introduce me, and he did so with the most colorful of language. As I say, he and I became friends, and as a result of all this Max became my client.

There were a number of cases that I handled for Max Adloff, but the most ambitious, the most rewarding, and the most fun was our suit against the Houston cemeteries for not allowing Max Adloff to place his monuments in various cemeteries because of their rule that *they* sold monuments and only *their* monuments could be used at your cemetery plot. We claimed that this practice was an illegal tie, as defined by the Sherman Antitrust Act-*i.e.*, in order to buy the lot, you also had to agree to buy the monument from the cemetery. We won this lawsuit and changed the practice of cemeteries all over America.

It was somewhere in this time frame that Max related to me one of the most devastating stories I have ever heard. He said that one day his young and only son was riding with him up the Old Katy Road on their way to Sealy, Texas. As Max and his son approached the long bridge that crossed the Brazos River in the lowlands, Max and his son saw a little dog run out in front of oncoming traffic, and it was hit by a truck.

At his son's urging, Max stopped the car on the bridge, and his young son opened the door and, before Max could warn him, ran to pick up the dying dog. As the little boy reached the dog, a truck, going in the same direction as Max's car, swerved around Max's car and struck his little boy carrying the dog. Max's son was killed instantly. And my friend Max picked up his dead son and carried him to the nearest hospital, probably in Brookshire, but it was too late. Max's life was ruined forever.

Shortly before Max died, years later, he told me that he was ready to join his little boy, who he believed was in the very next room.

During those years after Korea, I handled many general litigation cases. I represented banks and also became a condemnation lawyer,

BACK TO JOE'S LAW CAREER AND HOUSTON I.S.D.

representing landowners. One I particularly remember was when I represented George Page in a case of a boundary dispute involving a chicken coop against S. J. Kellen Construction Co. Col. Robert Sonfield was on the other side. During the trial of that case, I had called as my witness the county surveyor, Red Washburn, who testified that the chicken coop was not on the developer's property but that the developer was in fact trespassing over Page's land. Red Washburn made a great witness for me.

Then when Col. Sonfield began his cross-examination of Red, he asked Red if he had done all of the work on the survey. When Red said "no," Sonfield said "Who were the other surveyors?" Red said "Joe Blow" [fictitious name], and Col. Sonfield then asked, "Where is Joe Blow today and why isn't he the one testifying here?" Red answered the question by saying, "Sir, Joe Blow is in Korea fighting the Communists."

At that point Judge Campbell asked me, "Joe Reynolds, did you run into Joe Blow when you were over in Korea fighting with General MacArthur in the Marine Corps?" At which point Sonfield became irate. He jumped up and said, "I object, Your Honor. That is improper." And the judge said, "Well, Joe, you objected to it, too, didn't you? You objected to fighting in Korea, didn't you?"

Guess what? The jury ruled in my favor, though not for a lot of money, and of course, Sonfield appealed. The court of appeals ruled in my favor. And then Sonfield applied for a hearing before the Supreme Court of Texas, and the writ Supreme Court denied it.

After that *Page* case had been ruled on by the Supreme Court of Texas, Joe Greenhill called me and said, "Joe, there's no way you could have lost that case."

My life took a monumental change in 1956, when the NAACP sued the Houston Independent School District to integrate the Houston

◀ TOUCHED BY GRACE

public schools, under the doctrine of *Brown v. Board of Education*. Because of my experience in the *Sweatt* case while in the Attorney General's office, the school district approached me, a young, inexperienced lawyer, to be its counsel. The next 13 years made me famous or infamous, depending on your point of view. The name of this case was *Delores Ross v. Houston Independent School District*, and it fell into the federal court of Judge Ben Connally, one of the great trial judges in America.

This case started off with controversy. The papers were full of it. All school board meetings were televised, and everybody in Houston was tuned in. At the very first hearing, after the court was called to order, Judge Connally, with fire in his eyes, snarled at me, a man he'd never seen before, and said, "Counsel, stand up." I did. Judge Connally continued, "I want to ask you a direct question. Is it true that your clients, as reported in the paper, take the position that they will defy my orders and go to jail rather than integrate the Houston public schools?"

Still standing, I said, "Your Honor, as long as I'm the lawyer for the Houston public schools, I guarantee you that the school district will not only carry out the letter of your orders, but the spirit as well. And every member of the school board sits here in this courtroom, and they've authorized me to tell you that we will comply completely with the rulings of this court."

As I said, life changed for me as a result of this case. For the next nine years, I lived with Judge Connally. There were many appeals, many rulings, and I can only hit the highlights here. But in order to comply with the *Brown* doctrine, Joe Kelly Butler, President of our school board, or I, or Judge Connally, came up with the splendid idea that we would like to integrate our schools by integrating one grade a year, starting with kindergarten, coupled with giving every student in those grades the freedom of choice to go to any school they desired. After months of testimony, Judge Connally stated in June of

BACK TO JOE'S LAW CAREER AND HOUSTON I.S.D.

1960 that he would enter an order sometime that summer. We all held our bated breaths. Sometime in August of that summer, the Reynolds clan went to Colorado, where I unfortunately broke my right wrist trying to crank a bulldozer with a hand crank. Two days after this unfortunate accident, I got a call from Judge Connally's clerk, telling me to "get back to Houston immediately." Susie drove night and day, as my right arm was in a cast from the hand to the shoulder. (See the medical chapter for interesting story about that.)

I arrived in court together with my clients, and half of Houston, to hear the judge announce that he had approved our grade-a-year plan. We rejoiced. The NAACP did no rejoicing. They thought we were abusing the concept of "all deliberate speed," mandated in the *Brown* opinion.

That night I went home to calls from the newspapers every hour, and to Mama Sue and Hunt asking me questions I couldn't answer. Then I received a phone call from the Clerk of the Supreme Court of the United States! This was not a call from a secretary or other underling, but the clerk himself, to me, Joe Reynolds, at my home at night, advising me that I would appear not in court, but at the coffee shop at the New Orleans airport the following morning at ten o'clock, to meet Mr. Justice Rives of the Fifth Circuit and the lawyer for the NAACP, my friend Thurgood Marshall, to argue whether or not the Fifth Circuit would stay Judge Connally's order. Judge Connally had not entered a written order. Nobody had filed any written motion. There were no briefs. So far, everything was oral.

After notifying my clients, I caught the early morning flight to New Orleans, sat in a busy coffee shop at Moisant Airport, and met Judge Rives for the first time. The three of us were sitting in a booth, as Thurgood Marshall and I sat side by side facing the judge. Judge Rives asked us to present our positions and said, "Mr. Marshall, you go first."

TOUCHED BY GRACE

Mr. Marshall stated that it was incredible that 13 years to desegregate the Houston schools met the standard of "all deliberate speed." He had a point. My argument was that we had one of the great school systems of America, we had the support of the community, and that by giving the students in these grades freedom of choice, we would accomplish more than any school district in the north, and that all would be a free-will decision. After a couple of hours of give and take, Judge Rives told me to tell Judge Connally that he was throwing it back in his court, and it was Judge Connally's decision to make. We were right back where we started. And there was still nothing in writing, with the start of the school year imminent.

I rushed to catch the flight to Houston, knowing that Judge Connally was to be in Laredo federal court that afternoon. As I sat on that airplane, I was a nervous wreck. I had not had time to call anybody or plan anything. I became desperate. Finally, I knocked on the cockpit door and asked the pilot if he could send an emergency message to Judge Connally. He laughed at me! He told me that "nobody could do that." I begged. I pleaded. And finally he said, "let's give it a try." Via radio, I reported to Judge Connally, and he told me it was my problem, not his, and that he was on his way to Laredo. We interpreted that to mean that the schools would open tomorrow with our plan. But we weren't sure.

We arrived at the airport with all kinds of federal people wanting to know what in the world we were doing using that Delta radio for other than flying the airplane. I thought I was going to jail, but they relented. That night, Judge Connally called me from Laredo, and in a jovial voice, he asked me, "How'd it go?" Sufficeth to say, two days later the Houston schools were in the national press, since it was the largest segregated school district in the world, and it was starting its grade-a-year plan to integrate.

It should be noted that in 1956, when I took on this job of representing HISD, I immediately became a TV celebrity. There were only three TV stations in Houston, the NBC affiliate (Channel 2) and the CBS affiliate (Channel 11), and Channel 8, a joint-owned station of the University of Houston and Houston Independent School District. Every Monday night, from 7 p.m. until the wee hours of the morning, the school board meetings were televised, with UH providing the expertise and HISD providing the money. We had the largest audience of any program in Houston.

Every meeting was a war! Our Nielsen ratings were the highest of any station. The papers fanned the controversy. The liberal school board members snapped at the conservatives. The conservatives snapped back at the liberals. There was no middle ground. The *Houston Post* took the side of the liberals; the *Houston Chronicle* took the side of the conservatives; and every issue was hard-fought.

My role was to defend HISD in all of its lawsuits. There were many. At these televised school board meetings, I had to explain the "why" to every question. Every school superintendent, every school administrator, every school teacher within a hundred miles was glued to these programs. In all modesty, I had become a celebrity. But what really made me look good was that I normally had a pretty good idea of what Judge Connally was going to do.

One of the most interesting occurrences was when the federal government attempted to intervene. I don't recall the year, but I do recall that the Justice Department filed a motion to intervene, and before the motion was acted upon by the court, Judge Connally called a chambers conference with Weldon Berry, the attorney for the plaintiff, and me. When we arrived at Judge Connally's office, Washington attorney John Dorr, heading the Civil Rights Division of the Justice Department, entered at the same time. When Judge Connally's secretary told us to go into the judge's chambers, Mr. Dorr entered with us.

Judge Connally asked Mr. Dorr, "Who are you and what are you doing here?" Mr. Dorr identified himself and explained to the judge that on behalf of the Justice Department, he had filed a motion to intervene on behalf of the plaintiff, NAACP. Judge Connally said, "Counsel, I have not granted your motion to intervene. I have not even read it, and you are not welcome in my chambers. Get out."

After the door closed behind Dorr, Weldon Berry, perhaps facetiously, said to the judge, "Judge, if you allow the senior black boys at San Jacinto High School to wear mustaches, we would drop this case." I moved that the judge grant them that right. Judge Connally threw us out of his chambers.

During this time, the Houston School District was growing by leaps and bounds. Houston was the oil center of the world. Houston was the fastest-growing city in the world. Our schools were good, and our school population had increased rapidly by approximately 50,000 students. This increase necessitated the building of an additional 50 schools. This entailed bond work, condemnation of land, construction contracts, architects, and mountains of legal work, together with supervising and evaluating the desegregation lawsuit. I had to hire more lawyers. I was a busy man.

Our school board president, Joe Kelly Butler, a brilliant and gifted person, determined that the best plan would be to build the elementary schools in neighborhoods where people lived, and to build secondary schools on the boundaries of communities, so as to facilitate integration, such as a new Lincoln High School, bordering River Oaks on the west and the Fourth Ward on the east. This was the obvious plan to promote integration. But the NAACP didn't see it that way, and they filed another lawsuit, using different lawyers, to enjoin the implementation of this building program.

Judge Connally refused to allow this new case to be combined or consolidated with the *Dolores Ross* case. By the luck of the draw,

BACK TO JOE'S LAW CAREER AND HOUSTON I.S.D.

this new case fell in Judge Allen B. Hannay's court. (God help the NAACP.) At the conclusion of the preliminary injunction hearing, Judge Hannay announced that he and his entourage, together with the attorneys, would visit key locations and decide for himself whether this plan was racially motivated or whether it was for the purpose of complying with the *Brown* doctrine. The tour began.

Our first stop was at E.O. Smith Junior High School. It was a harbinger of things to come. As the entourage moved into the entrance of E.O. Smith, following in Judge Hannay's wake, the principal, a black man, came forward to meet Judge Hannay. As the two reached each other, they embraced and started crying! Without a word to any of us, the two of them proceeded to a conference room, and we followed, where we all sat down. Then Judge Hannay and the principal became aware that the rest of us were present. Judge Hannay announced for our edification that he and the principal had grown up together as little boys in Hempstead, Texas; the principal's grandfather had been the slave of Judge Hannay's grandfather, and the two of them were like brothers.

After this explanation, Judge Hannay asked the principal what he thought of the HISD building program. The principal's response was, "Your Honor, it is a great program. We have a great school district. We will continue to have a great school district. And this plan will comply with the requirements of *Brown* and maintain the integrity and the quality of all our schools."

School, for this lawsuit, was out.

Our next stop was McReynolds Junior High out on the east side, near Canal Street. My recollection is that all of the entourage, plus the press, were invited to lunch at McReynolds Junior High. By this time, Mr. Dorr was hanging onto me, because I was the only friend he had in the city. I recall Elmer Bertleson, the *Chronicle* reporter, pulling up a chair at the end of the table, and sitting next to Dorr, who was sitting next to me, and asking Mr. Dorr: "Sir, are you married?"

Mr. Dorr answered "yes."

"Well how many children do you have?"

"Five."

"Do they go to integrated schools?"

Silence.

"Do they go to public school?"

Silence.

And Bertleson of the *Chronicle* responded, "I take it by your silence that your children go to a segregated, private school. Is that right?

Mr. Dorr hung his head and said, "Yes."

Mr. Bertleson said, "This is news, and it will be properly reported."

And so it was.

The final aspect of this second case was when the NAACP appealed the case to the Fifth Circuit, where the panel was comprised of Judge John Brown , Judge Tuttle, and, believe it or not, Judge Ben Connally. When I argued for the school district, Judge Tuttle said, "Joe, before you start, I want to ask you a question." And Judge Brown said, "Joe, before you answer Judge Tuttle's question, I want you to answer mine."

BACK TO JOE'S LAW CAREER AND HOUSTON I.S.D.

For the next 20 minutes, I answered questions that were served to me like a pitcher in batting practice. Then when Joe Teta, for the NAACP, argued, he felt the wrath and fury of Judge Connally, who all but accused him and the NAACP of having filed a bad-faith lawsuit, when any person of common intelligence should have known that this plan was designed intentionally to help promote desegregation in the Houston School District. The Fifth Circuit opinion affirming Judge Hannay was anticlimactic.

In 1969, because integration had worked so well and had been received so well, I moved on behalf of the school district that the four remaining grades be desegregated simultaneously beginning with the next school year. And so ended one of the most dramatic eras in Houston's history.

In all truthfulness, integration of the Houston public schools became a model for the rest of America. However, on the day I resigned as the attorney for the school district, Mrs. Hattie Mae White, the black member of the school board, walked over to me and stuck her finger in my face, telling me that I had personally caused her daughter to receive an inferior education. As politely as I knew how, I asked Mrs. White if she knew what the term "racist" meant. After she didn't answer, I told her that a racist was a person who made decisions based on race, and that I was not the racist in that room.

Two days later, Mrs. White called me and apologized, and told me she would like for me to be her lawyer if she ever needed one. In later years, I had the privilege of helping this black woman through some very trying times.

Parenthetically, these 13 years representing the Houston public schools, and by this time nearly every school district in Texas and some in other states, allowed me to become one of the best-known lawyers in Texas. My law firm, which began as Reynolds, White,

◄ TOUCHED BY GRACE

Allen & Cook, prospered and grew from seven lawyers in the '60s to 120 when the firm dissolved in May of 1988, occasioned in part by my heart surgery.

During the school years, I did indeed do the legal work for about 20 school districts in Texas. I could easily have specialized in School Law, but that was not what I wanted to do. Even so, some of the other school cases are worth remembering.

BLACK SCHOOL TEACHERS V. ANAHUAC INDEPENDENT SCHOOL DISTRICT

Years before this case came into being, I had met a man I admired very much. He was a young school superintendent at Anahuac, a small town in Southeast Texas along the Gulf coast, named Hank Wheeler. Hank was in the forefront of modern school education in Texas, and Susie and I got to know Hank and his family very well. We became close friends. Our friendship began during Texas's desegregation period. It was at this time that the Anahuac School District decided that it would unitize its schools. This meant that the black students, who had formerly gone to separate schools, would now go to school with white students and vice-versa. It also meant that faculty would be integrated among the schools.

Hank was Anahuac School District's superintendent. A part of the Anahuac plan was to select the teachers not on a basis of race but on a basis of ability, and as they consolidated the system, some three or four black teachers were let go because of a surplus of teachers. This was done after a very careful analysis by the superintendent and the school board working together.

Of course, the NAACP sued. In this case the NAACP was represented by a lawyer named Larry Watts. I had known Larry Watts for a number of years. He is a lawyer who is younger than I, and who appeared to be a buffoon. I had known him in an Aldine case; I had known him in connection with my representation of a

BACK TO JOE'S LAW CAREER AND HOUSTON I.S.D.

football coach at Fort Stockton, Texas; and I had met him on other occasions in other cases. But now he was lead counsel in the case of the black teachers versus Anahuac ISD.

Watts filed his case, and it landed in Judge Noel's court, a federal district judge for the Southern District of Texas in Houston. The case was set for trial, and in this instance there was no jury. I met in the courtroom with Hank, and we were there to defend the case. For his first witness, Watts called his expert (a man whose name I cannot recall). The expert was a disaster for him.

This initial witness for the NAACP began his testimony on Friday, and he invented quotations from other experts. Over the weekend, the judge himself went to the Rice Library and read these authorities quoted by this expert, and came back Monday morning and proceeded to grill Watts' expert, devastating the witness because of his plagiarism. That, however, is not the point of this story.

The point of this story is that the next witness called by Watts was my own school board president, Mr. Ocie Jackson. I had known Mr. Jackson for some time, and I liked him very much. He was a quiet, soft-spoken man, and he had been very instrumental in working out the unitization plan for Anahuac ISD.

Mr. Jackson was sworn by the clerk to tell the truth, the whole truth, and nothing but the truth, and he took the witness stand. Watts began his cross-examination (Mr. Jackson being a "hostile witness" to Watts), and it went something like this:

Watts:	*State your name, please.*
Jackson:	*Jackson*
Watts:	*Where do you live?*
Jackson:	*Anahuac, Texas.*
Watts:	*Are you a member of the Anahuac School Board?*
Jackson:	*Yes, I am.*

Watts:	How long have you been a member of that school board?
Jackson:	Approximately 20 years.
Watts:	Are you currently the president of that school board?
Jackson:	Yes, I am.
Watts:	How long have you been president of that school board?
Jackson:	Many years.
Watts:	Were you involved in the unitization plan with Mr. Wheeler?
Jackson:	Yes, I was.
Watts:	Did you play a significant part?
Jackson:	Well, I think I did.
Watts:	Isn't it true, Mr. Jackson, that you and you alone made the decision to terminate these black teachers?
Jackson:	No, Sir; that is not true.
Watts:	Isn't it true, Sir, that you made the ultimate decision to fire these black teachers?
Jackson:	No, I did not do that, but we tried to hire and keep the very best teachers, regardless of race.
Watts:	Isn't it true, Mr. Jackson, that you, as president of this school board over the years, have deliberately terminated black teachers and you deliberately maintained a segregated school system because you were opposed to integration?
Jackson:	No, that is not true.

At this juncture, as Watts' voice got more and more hostile toward the witness, Judge Noel interrupted. Judge Noel looked down to Mr. Jackson and said, "Mr. Jackson, look up here at me, please." The witness looked at Judge Noel. Judge Noel then said, "Mr. Jackson, how long have you known me?"

The witness said, "Judge, I've known you longer than 20 years."

The judge said to Mr. Jackson, "How many times over the last number of years have you served as foreman of my grand jury?"

Mr. Jackson said, "Well, Judge, I think three or four times at least."

Then the judge looked at him and said, "Mr. Jackson, just for the record, state your race."

Mr. Jackson very quietly said, "I am a Negro."

Watts turned purple. He could have qualified for a Code Blue. He looked horrible. I thought he was about to have a heart attack. He was absolutely stunned. Mr. Jackson, of course, didn't look black, but I knew that he was a Negro. Everyone respected him, and he was an outstanding school board president.

The judge asked Watts, "Do you have any further questions of this witness?" Watts said "No."

The judge said, "Mr. Watts, do you have anything else you wish to offer the court?" Watts said "No."

The judge ruled in Anahuac's favor.

The Riesel School District Case in Waco

The case of *Houston Fire & Casualty Insurance Company v. Riesel Independent School District* (tried as *Riesel Independent School District v. Houston Fire & Casualty Insurance Company*), 375 S.W.2d 323 [Tex. App.—Waco 1964, writ ref'd, n.r.e.]) was an unusual and significant case.

In late 1958 or early 1959, Murray Watson, who was a state representative from McLennan County, contacted me, because he had learned that I represented the Houston School District. Murray had signed up a contingent fee case with the Riesel Independent School District for a suit against the contractor that built an entirely new school in Riesel, a little town about 20 miles south of Waco on Hwy. 6, in 1955, and its bonding company.

The building had been terribly constructed and could not be repaired to a proper condition. The contract price was $310,000. I filed the lawsuit shortly before the statute of limitations ran out on the claim. The contractor was nowhere to be found, and we obtained a default judgment against it for $210,000.

I then handed the case off to one of the young lawyers at Bracewell Reynolds & Patterson, and nobody did anything with it as it was handed down over a period of about three years from each lawyer to the next youngest one on the list.

When Grant Cook came to work for me in March 1961, no discovery had taken place in the case, nor had any other activity occurred in it following the default judgment. Grant had just graduated from Baylor Law School, so I thought that he would like to take over the case and work it up for trial with me, because that would get him back to Waco (little did I know that he had no interest whatsoever in ever going back to Waco).

In any event, Grant took the case and found an expert witness and a couple of fact witnesses. Bear in mind that this was six years after, and anybody who really knew anything about the contract and the construction of the school was very hard to find. I promised Grant that we would work the case up together and try it together. No depositions or any written discovery were ever done.

It came up for trial in February 1962. On Sunday afternoon before the trial was to begin on Monday, Grant drove us to Waco while I read through the file. I had not looked at the file probably since one of my young associates had gotten a default judgment several years earlier.

During the trip, Grant told me about the witnesses he had lined up to testify and the expert, and it all sounded good until I asked him how we were going to prove our damages. Grant promptly told me that the damages in a case like this were the cost of repair of the defects if they could be repaired without "substantial alteration to the structure as a whole" and if not, the damages would be the difference between the contract price and the present value of the school building. Since repair was not possible, he said that the latter was the correct measure of damages.

When I asked him how he was going to prove the present value of the school building, he told me that he hadn't even though of that but just assumed that it wouldn't be much.

Grant and I shared a small motel room on Waco Drive Sunday night and when we got up to get dressed to go to court on Monday morning, the first thing I learned was that I had forgotten to bring my shoes, as I had been wearing my house slippers on Sunday afternoon when I left my house. So we went to court and got word to the judge that I had to wait until the stores opened so I could buy a pair of shoes and the judge kindly gave us a 30-minute continuance.

The biggest problem we had at the start of the trial was that Grant had not secured an expert witness to testify on the value of the school building as it was built. We were drinking coffee in the basement of the courthouse on the first day and I noticed an office sign down the hall of the "County School Superintendent."

We went down there, I introduced myself to the gentleman, and asked him if he was aware of the condition of the Riesel school building and he said that he was. I then asked him what he thought it was worth. He said he had no idea. I told him that it was probably worth something for salvage value, and he agreed. We decided that it was worth $100,000, meaning our damages were $210,000.

The next day we put him on the witness stand as an expert witness and he so testified (this was before you had to reveal everything about your expert witnesses before trial).

I decided to divide the task of the trial by letting Grant put on our case, and I would cross-examine their witnesses, principally because I did not know a great deal about the facts, even after having reviewed the file.

Fortunately for all of us, the facts were pretty straightforward. The contractor had done a horrible job constructing the school building, and particularly the foundation. The architect designed and the contractor followed a fixed pier and beam foundation plan, which was totally unacceptable in the clay underlying Riesel.

The result was that as the ground shifted, the foundation held firm and all of the walls made of concrete blocks began to crack. This made most of the doors inoperable and generally ruined the building.

The high point of the testimony during the trial occurred when the defense lawyer, Smith, of the fine old Waco firm of Naman, Howell & Smith, was cross-examining our engineer expert witness, who had expressed his opinion that the contractor did not build the building in accordance with good and workmanlike standards nor in accordance with the plans and specifications in all respects.

That witness was a good-looking young man about the size of a defensive lineman. On cross-examination, Mr. Smith got in the witness's face to conclude his cross-examination by saying, "Are you trying to make this jury believe that that school out there is about to fall down and kill a bunch of children?" To which the witness replied, "shooooot no."

Mr. Smith passed the witness and turned on his heel to his counsel table, when the witness looked directly over at the jury and said, "But I sure wouldn't want my little girls going to school in that building." That pretty much cinched the lawsuit.

The trial lasted until Friday. When we got down to the jury argument, I told Grant that he could open, and I would close. One of the most significant legal and factual issues in the case was whether or not the school district had received a "completion certificate" from the architect before they paid the contractor the full amount of the contract.

The bonding company took the position that if there was such a certificate, the architect's approval cut off the ability of the school district to bring suit for faulty construction and, if the school board did not receive the certificate, they breached the contract (to which the bonding company was a third party beneficiary) by reason of paying the contractor in the absence of such a certificate of completion by the architect.

Now, I know that sounds like a bunch of lawyer talk, but let me just say that there was no case law directly on point. The only facts that came out in the trial on the subject were that one of the school district employees testified that he "thought" that he had seen the architect's completion certificate in the superintendent's file some years before, but had looked for it and couldn't find it. Otherwise, there was no evidence as to whether or not the architect ever issued a completion certificate.

Grant believed that our best legal position was that a certificate had in fact been issued, but I thought it would be better if the jury found that it had not been issued. We had not agreed on that at the time Grant began making his argument.

In those days, lawyers would write the answers on a blackboard that they wanted the jury to give to the special issues. Grant did so and on the architect's certificate issue, asked the jury to find "Yes" that such a certificate was issued. I was incensed.

After the defense lawyers made their argument, I got up to close. The first thing I did was tell the jury that Grant was a very young lawyer right out of Baylor Law School and that I thought he had done a fine job in the case-except that he had given them the wrong answer to the question concerning the architect's certificate.

So I erased the "Yes" that Grant had written on the board and filled in "No."

The jury went out late in the afternoon and deliberated until almost midnight. The verdict came back exactly as we wanted with the jury finding the issue on the architect's completion certificate the way I told them-that is, that it had not been issued. More importantly, they found the damages exactly as we had asked, $210,000. That was the largest verdict in the history of McLennan County as of that date.

Grant finally convinced me that he was right with respect to our best legal position concerning the architect's completion certificate, and I gave him permission to ask the judge to disregard that jury finding and enter a judgment in our favor, which the court did, resulting in a $210,000 judgment which, like the verdict, was the largest judgment in the history of McLennan County at that time.

Of course, the bonding company appealed, and Judge Frank Wilson of the Waco Court of Appeals (probably one of the most venerated appellate judges in Texas) wrote an opinion affirming our judgment, and the Supreme Court refused to review it. We finally got the money in the summer of 1968, and it resulted in the biggest single fee paid to my law firm that year.

CHAPTER 9

Joe's Career Shifts To High Gear

"I Led Four Lives"
- *family man*
  - *lawyer*
    - *regent*
      - *trustee*

During the hectic days of *Ross*, I had another fabulous experience. In 1957, then-Attorney General of Texas Will Wilson called me and told me he would like to hire me as a Special Assistant Attorney General to represent the State of Texas against all of the electrical contractors in the Gulf Coast area and their labor unions.

After much study and briefing on behalf of the State, I filed a Texas antitrust case against the electrical contractors and the labor union, in state court, claiming that the contractors and labor unions were dividing up the business with rigged bids, enforced by the union. The attorneys representing the defendants sounded like Who's Who Among the American Bar.

First was Colonel Leon Jaworski representing one of the defendants. Then came Jack Binion, of the great law firm of Butler & Binion, representing another defendant. Also representing a defendant was the great antitrust lawyer, perhaps one of the greatest in America, Leroy Jeffers of Vinson & Elkins. A fourth was Tom Phillips of Baker & Botts, another of the leading antitrust lawyers in America. Representing the labor union was a lawyer named J. Edwin Smith, who was considered one of the top trial labor lawyers in America.

I was up against the cream of the crop. All these lawyers were my senior by at least 25 years. They were among the great lawyers of America, and without doubt, were the top lawyers of Houston and Texas. Despite the differences in age, experience, and ability, they treated me as an equal. When I tell this story, lawyers don't believe it, but it's true. Not only did they treat me as an equal, they treated me with a courtesy that developed into friendship.

After much discovery, the trial judge, Ben Wilson, without ever allowing my argument to soak in but being totally awed by my opponents, granted the defendants' summary judgment on the grounds that federal antitrust laws had preempted state antitrust laws. I appealed to the First Court of Appeals sitting in Houston. The judges on the court of appeals panel consisted of Judge Tom Coleman, Judge Spurgeon Bell, and Judge Bill Hamblen, three of the most eminent appellate judges in Texas.

I got to open and close oral argument. In between my two arguments, these paragons eloquently presented their case, and as I finished my closing argument, Tom Phillips turned to the other defense lawyers and said, "Which of us is going to write the motion for rehearing?" He was right in his assumption that I was going to win. The court of appeals in a unanimous decision held for my client. They later took the case to the United States Supreme Court, but justice prevailed-which means I won.

JOE'S CAREER SHIFTS TO HIGH GEAR

It was after the appellate court argument that these fine lawyers got together and jointly recommended me for membership in the American College of Trial Lawyers. And in August of 1962, along with Curtiss Brown, I was inaugurated into this august organization.

I can't leave this story without telling an incident that occurred immediately following the induction service. Colonel Jaworski was president of the American College the summer I was inducted, and Mr. Justice Tom Clark of the Supreme Court of the United States was the speaker at the induction.

As we left the elaborate ceremony at the Mark Hopkins Hotel in San Francisco, Colonel Jaworski put his arm around my shoulder and walked with me to the entrance of the hotel. As we stood there before the revolving door, Mr. Justice Clark approached Colonel Jaworski, and Colonel Jaworski introduced me as "one of the gifted young lawyers of Houston."

He told Mr. Justice Clark that I had just won a very important case in federal court in Houston before Judge Connally, where I represented the Houston public schools, in which case Judge Connally ruled that prayer in the public schools was not unconstitutional. Mr. Justice Clark put his arm also around my shoulder, and I stood there being hugged by these two renowned jurists. Mr. Justice Clark said, "Joe," (as if I were his long-time friend) "let me tell you something. As long as I am on the Supreme Court of the United States, there will always be prayer in the public schools of America."

I was thrilled! I was ecstatic. I was beside myself. That meant I would win my case on appeal, and I couldn't wait to get back to tell Judge Connally. The first day back in Houston, I called Judge Connally to take him to lunch. We met at the Lancaster Hotel. Before we even ordered our food, I told him this wonderful story and what Mr. Justice Clark had said to me. Judge Connally took his glasses off and looked at me and said, "Joe, did you believe him?"

◀ TOUCHED BY GRACE

I was stunned! I was shocked. I was speechless. But three months later, the Supreme Court of the United States wrote an opinion involving a school district in New York, holding that prayer in public schools of America was unconstitutional. The opinion was written by Mr. Justice Tom Clark.

One of the significant things about the above story is that these five men thereafter included me in their little circle of friendly lawyers. You cannot imagine what this did for me. Jack Binion offered me a job with Butler & Binion. Colonel Jaworski asked me to hire his son and teach him to be a lawyer with my ethics, which I did. Leroy Jeffers sent me lawsuits. Tom Phillips became my very good friend and referred me cases, and he told my friend Joe Greenhill that he (Greenhill) had created a Frankenstein!

I want to talk here a little bit about judges who have influenced my career, starting with Carl Bue, a retired federal judge who is still my good friend this day in 2009 as I finally am completing this book. Carl Bue officed "down the hall" in the same building as I did, the old San Jacinto Building on Main Street in downtown Houston, when I was a lawyer with Bracewell & Tunks. He and I became very close friends.

We were both interested in history, and we both loved Winston Churchill and Douglas MacArthur. Many a night Susie and I would go to their house, where Carl and I would sit on his front porch swing and listen to Churchill speeches, as Mary and Susie would visit and then drop off to sleep. After Carl and I had listened to Churchill on many tapes, we would wake up the girls and Susie and I would go home.

Early on, Carl was appointed a federal judge in the Southern District of Texas, and he was one of the most intelligent judges I had ever come before. He knew the rules of evidence, he understood how to prepare a charge, and he was a specialist in antitrust laws. He was indeed a gifted judge.

JOE'S CAREER SHIFTS TO HIGH GEAR

Along about the same time, my friend John Singleton became a federal judge. John had been a lawyer with Fulbright, and John had tried lots of lawsuits. He was indeed a character. He was not the brain that Carl was, but he had the best sense of humor of any judge in the federal system. Being in his court was a lot of fun, and there was never a dull day. In the famous "corrugated box" antitrust case, in which there were about 20 trial lawyers, he allowed the jury each day to select their favorite lawyer and their *least* favorite lawyer. Most of the lawyers won both contests at one time or another.

When the box case was over, and my side had won, I discovered that the mother of a lady juror from LaGrange, Texas, was Joe Hart's secretary. Joe Hart was my buddy from the Marines, and we tried bunches of lawsuits together in LaGrange. In fact, the juror's mother told me later, "Mr. Reynolds, there was no way you were gonna lose that case." Little did I know.

While on the subject of judges, I should mention Judge Ingraham. Judge Ingraham and I became close friends during Eisenhower's campaign for President, and I believe it was Eisenhower who appointed Judge Ingraham to the federal bench. But after he became a judge, he called me one day to tell me that he had just read an opinion from a Louisiana court that had outlawed the playing of the song *Dixie,* and he wanted me to intervene and represent St. John the Baptiste Parish and to "get that case reversed." In fact, he demanded it.

About two years later, after he had been appointed to the Fifth Circuit Court of Appeals, a friend called to ask if I had read Judge Ingraham's first opinion as an appellate judge. And my friend promptly delivered to me Judge Ingraham's first opinion, which outlawed the singing of *Dixie* in the Florida school districts! Judge Ingraham would never discuss a case with me after that. But he still remained my friend.

I remember one time getting a call from Judge Hannay. It was shortly after Lyndon Johnson had become President. Judge Hannay called me to come to his chambers. He was livid. John Singleton had just left his chambers and had requested that Judge Hannay retire, so that "Lyndon" could appoint John to Judge Hannay's place on the bench. Judge Hannay was not a happy camper. But since I was *persona non grata* with Lyndon Johnson, I could do little more than empathize with my friend Judge Hannay.

Judge Hannay continued to serve with distinction for several more years. And he wrote a very important opinion for those of us who are Texas history knowledge-seekers. I have always called it the "Hannay Opinion." His opinion in the case of *Amaya v. Stanolind Oil & Gas Co.*, 62 F. Supp. 181 (S.D. Tx. 1945), concerns the ownership of all Texas land west of the Nueces River that was claimed by Mexico, whose citizens were dispossessed of the property after the Battle of San Jacinto. For readers who are not Texans, that famous 21-minute battle was won by the Texas Army under Sam Houston, after the brave men of the Alamo had held off Santa Anna for 13 glorious days. The result of the victory at San Jacinto was Texas independence.

After his defeat, General Santa Anna signed a document agreeing that the boundary of Mexico and Texas was the Rio Grande Del Norte, or the Rio Grande River. Even after the Mexican-American War, the treaty of Guadalupe Hidalgo in 1848 confirmed that boundary. Yet some Mexican citizens still tried to dispute it in Judge Hannay's court in 1945.

Judge Hannay ruled that the Mexican citizens had no claim to that land, and in that "Hannay Opinion" he recounts the Battle of San Jacinto, and specifically recounts the meeting and conversation between Sam Houston and Santa Anna at the conclusion of the battle.

The opinion states that the battle of San Jacinto was the 16th most decisive battle in the history of the world, resulting in the annihilation of the Mexican Army, the capture of the Mexican President Santa Anna, and the independence of Texas, which led to the founding of the Republic of Texas. There's no telling how many times I've had Carol copy that opinion and send it to somebody for me.

CHAPTER **10**

The Tenneco Years

Tenneco was a large conglomerate corporation, the third largest company in Houston, that was leading the Houston economy in the days of the oil boom that so invigorated the city. From the early '60s and for some 30 years, I was the outside trial counsel for Tenneco. How Tenneco became my client is a long and interesting story, involving many interesting connections and people.

Vernon Turner, General Counsel of the oil company, was my lifetime friend. Milton Covey, Company Secretary, and I had grown up in Tyler together and had gone to law school together. Last but not least, Clyde Wilson, the famous private eye and also head of Tenneco Security, was my good buddy. But Mr. Freeman, President and Chief Executive Officer, called the shots. My cases for Tenneco are too numerous to detail here, but some were real humdingers!

Very early on Vernon engaged me to represent Tenneco in a case involving a breach of a drilling contract in which Tenneco had leased a ship and rig to drill a fairly deep oil well in the North Sea. The amounts involved were huge for those days. Tenneco had agreed to pay $15,000 a day for rent of a jack-up rig. Due to the drilling contractor's negligence, after drilling a dry hole, the operator failed to lower the rig into the ship and to move it off of the site. Winter and weather set in, and so the rig sat idle in the North Sea for some 300 days, at $15,000 a day.

Vernon and I made a trip to Europe to investigate the facts. Venue for the case was at The Hague in the World Court. On that first trip to London, I settled the case with Tenneco paying only an insignificant amount of the claimed rental. It was a great settlement for Tenneco.

The morning after I returned to Houston, I got a call from Mr. Freeman. He was irate! He told me he could not believe I had settled his lawsuit. He said I was too stupid to be his lawyer. I tried to protest. In his customary fashion, he said, "Don't interrupt me. Let me finish." And then he said, "You still don't get it, do you?" And he added, "Reynolds, you had the opportunity to spend the rest of your life in Europe at my expense, but what do you do? You make one trip and settle. You're too dumb to be my lawyer." Then he laughed-and I got it.

Mr. Freeman and I had a remarkable friendship. Upon Mr. Freeman's demand, our law firm became the first tenant of the 1100 Milam Building in Houston, a downtown office building owned by Tenneco. One day Mr. Freeman came by, around 5 in the afternoon, barging in my office with a huge entourage. I was on the phone talking to Governor Briscoe. Mr. Freeman demanded that I hang up. I said, "Just a minute, I'm talking to Governor Briscoe."

He laughed loudly and told his entourage, "Reynolds is a name-dropper." I continued to talk. At that point, Mr. Freeman, with his usual impatience, grabbed the phone from my hand and loudly declared, "I am Dick Freeman. Who am I talking to?" His next words were classic. "Yes, Governor. Yes, Governor. Yes, Governor. That would be fine." And then he turned to me and quietly said,

THE TENNECO YEARS

"The Governor wants you to bring me to dinner tomorrow at the Governor's Mansion." Without another word, he took his entourage and left.

Stories about Mr. Freeman abound. For instance, there was the time I came home to my wife and found her in tears. Mr. Freeman had called and demanded that she find our last three income tax returns and that I deliver those to him personally, in his office, the next morning at 8 a.m. He made her believe that I was being investigated in some manner for overcharging Tenneco.

I arrived at his office the next morning a little before 8 and, without saying 'hello,' he asked if I had brought my tax returns as he had requested. I handed them to him. He quickly reviewed them and said, "Just as I thought. You are going to work for me as General Counsel at Tenneco, and you will be paid three times the average of these last three returns." I was dumfounded. But God gave me the words to say. "Mr. Freeman," I said, "nothing would please me more than being General Counsel of Tenneco. But if I became General Counsel, then I couldn't try your lawsuits, and I'm not sure that I could handle that. You and I have too much fun together at the courthouse." He said, "I never thought of that. Help me find another General Counsel."

Then there was the time I went into his office, and he told me abruptly that my law firm needed 30 more lawyers, we were going into the FERC business, and we needed lawyers. (FERC is the acronym for the Federal Energy Regulatory Commission, an independent governmental agency that regulates the interstate transmission of electricity, natural gas, and oil.) I said, "Mr. Freeman, I wouldn't know where to hire 30 FERC lawyers." And then with a string of expletives, he said, "Do you expect me to hire your lawyers for you also?"

Then he yelled at his secretary to get Gordon Gooch, head of Baker & Botts' Washington office, and said, "Gordon, you and your staff are leaving Baker, Botts today and going to work for Joe Reynolds and his law firm. I want him to have a Washington office, and he will represent and handle all of Tenneco's business." Gordon died a hundred deaths. Later, much to Mr. Freeman's displeasure, I let Gordon off the hook, but ultimately I opened a Washington office with the famous Bob Perdue handling Tenneco's FERC business. Charley Moore, one of my best litigators, later served as General Counsel of the FERC for a few years.

Or there was the time Mr. Freeman sent me to Kern County, California, to sue 20 Mule Team Borax (I'm reminded of Ronald Reagan hosting the old TV program, "Death Valley Days") over their depleting a borax mine that belonged to Tenneco. The mine was located at Furnace Creek in Death Valley-not exactly a garden spot of the California-Nevada border area.

I spent many nights and days in a run-down old motel, whose air conditioning system was woefully unfit, preparing to try the case at Riverside, California. In the meantime, Mr. Freeman was ensconced at the MGM Grand Hotel in Las Vegas. Once a month we made a trip. He remained in Las Vegas with the Tenneco plane, while I would rent a car and drive alone through heat and sand to my rendezvous at Furnace Creek.

Or then there was the time Mr. Freeman decided that I was the greatest labor lawyer in America. Obviously, I knew nothing about it. I was not a labor lawyer. But in a very murky problem, we sued Cesar Chavez and the United Farm Workers in Stockton, California. I won't bore you with the details of that lawsuit, except to say that the lawsuit and the Kern County problem kept me living in Bakersfield, California, for approximately a year. The highlight of the whole experience was that Mr. Freeman called Susie and asked her whether I liked turkey or ham. He was sending me one or the other for Christmas dinner at the Hill House in Bakersfield (also owned by Tenneco). Susie told me about that call and I went home for Christmas dinner.

THE TENNECO YEARS

The biggest case I ever handled for Tenneco was the famous *Air Products v. Tenneco*. Air Products sued Tenneco for several billion dollars. The allegations roughly were that Tenneco had breached its gas contract by refusing to deliver to Air Products all of the gas dedicated to Air Products by Tenneco, causing Air Products to be unable to fulfill its obligation to deliver fuel to launch Saturn rockets.

Our defense was simply that the federal government had interceded and was requiring us to send this fuel to warm the people in New York City. Over the period of a couple of years we spent lots of money, took lots of depositions, and there were 10 or 12 lawyers in the firm who spent their full time on *Air Products*. My role was to go to Allentown, Pennsylvania, every other week, rain, sleet, snow, or shine, to depose Air Products people.

On one occasion I was taking the deposition of Air Products' Dr. Wang, a real rocket scientist. He was the rudest man I ever met. My questions started around 9 in the morning, and for two hours he answered each of my questions with, "Your question is stupid," or "You are stupid," or "There's no way anyone can answer a stupid question like that, and obviously you don't understand anything about this business." After a while it got to me. I asked the court reporter to go off the record.

I then stood up and walked around the table to where Dr. Wang was sitting, and I reached over and grabbed him by the tie and literally lifted him out of his chair and stood him on his feet. The Air Products lawyer, Curtis Boisfontaine, didn't make a sound and didn't say a word.

I then told Dr. Wang, who was either Japanese or Chinese-or both- that "25 years ago I was killing little slant-eyes like you, and I'm fixing to start it again." Dr. Wang then begged my pardon, bowed at the waist, and for the next two hours was the best witness I ever had. Ironically, it was his testimony that allowed us to eventually settle this very big lawsuit.

◄ TOUCHED BY GRACE

But Tenneco's story would not be complete without mentioning my last case for Tenneco. It was after my heart operation. My law firm had dissolved, and Tenneco had sold the oil company for whom I had worked lo these many years. The officers of the oil company each had received a golden parachute, and they felt badly that I didn't get one. But there was no way.

And so they suggested that I handle one remaining case for the oil company, where their subsidiary, Houston Oil & Minerals, had a claim against Lone Star Gas for underpayment for gas contracted, and that I would handle this case on a modified contingent basis. This was something Tenneco had never done before. It was a good case, and we were fortunate to win, and we ultimately settled the case, allowing me to retire if I wanted, along with my Tenneco friends. Somehow I just didn't get around to retiring. but I'm working on it.

During many of these years that I represented Tenneco, I was also on the Board of Regents at Texas A&M University. During that time Mr. Freeman was President of the Houston Livestock Show & Rodeo. So naturally I became the lawyer for the Livestock Show on a *pro bono* basis.

Every year the Houston Livestock Show & rodeo put on the biggest rodeo in the world. It was held at the Astrodome, then known as the 8th Wonder of the World. Not only were there the standard rodeo events and competitions and exhibitors, but each night's show also featured a star performer-usually a singer or musical group. Many people came just to see the entertainers. It was my job to prepare the contracts with all of the stars with whom Mr. Freeman had negotiated.

I met some interesting people through what I sometimes still refer to as the "Fat Stock Show." One of them was a woman by the name of Juliet Prowse, whom Mr. Freeman-or rather, I-fired during her show. She had refused to shake hands with the little children at the dome stadium, and Mr. Freeman told me to kick her *&%> out of the dome.

An even better story is about the time Eddie Rabbit got sick, and Mr. Freeman heard of a young country-western singer down at Pleasanton, Texas, and sent us in the Tenneco plane to get him. We got him there just in time to get him on the stage. He didn't even have time to remove his hat. So the first time to my knowledge a country-western singer gave his performance wearing his Stetson hat, and this was the beginning of George Strait's fabulous career. Mr. Freeman, of course, explained to all who would listen that he discovered George Strait.

Finally, because of my relationship with Mr. Freeman, he arranged for the Houston Livestock Show & Rodeo to be the largest giver of scholarships to students attending Texas A&M. This was a mammoth contribution, not only to these young people, but also to A&M. For this service, I recommended that the horse facility, which is the best horse arena in Texas, be named for my boss and friend, N. W. "Dick" Freeman. And it bears his name to this day on the campus at Texas A&M University.

Mr. Freeman, a chain smoker, passed away with lung cancer several years ago. In fact, one of our most interesting conversations was the day I took him to the airport in my car, which had a red sign in it, "No Smoking," and he smoked all the way to the airport. And as he got out of the car, he said, "I know you didn't mean for that sign to apply to me."

He was a character. And either Clyde Wilson or I, or both of us, were with him everywhere he went. It was required of me to have lunch with him two or three times a week. We generally ate at Hugo's Window Box at the Hyatt Regency in downtown Houston.

The story of Tenneco cannot be complete without my reference to another outstanding officer, Joe Bill Foster. This man was a giant. Still is. He became my friend, my confidante, my benefactor. He is one of the finest men I ever met. Joe's lifestyle and mine are very much the same, and for approximately 20 years we played tennis together every Tuesday morning. And I think Mr. Freeman felt that Joe Foster and I were somehow related. In any event, it would be fair to say that together with Clyde Wilson, the other Joe and I were the Teacher's Pets.

Several years after Mr. Freeman's death, the oil company had been sold, and Joe Bill was about to leave for other pursuits. Joe Bill again did the unheard of and invited Susie and me to spend a week with Joe Bill and his wife and another couple on the Tenneco yacht in the Bahamas. After that wonderful trip, like that setting sun down there off of Bimini, Tenneco passed over the horizon. It remains only a memory for me and others.

CHAPTER 11

Meet Mr. Hess

At this point in our narrative, I need to say it is impossible to retry in this format every case I've tried over the last 60+ years. The number of tried jury cases must be between 350 and 400. In fact, someone told me that next to Henry Giessel, a local lawyer, I had tried more cases than any other lawyer in Texas. This may or may not be true. Many of these cases were never appealed, and many settled after several days of trial, but nearly all of them were very interesting and have their own story to tell. But, sadly, time does not permit.

My many condemnation cases for HISD and other school districts during the school boom days of Houston were legion. Likewise, my client Gibraltar Savings, the largest savings and loan in Texas, had the policy of trying all of their cases, without any possibility of settlement, so as to discourage nuisance cases from being filed against it. Only the Lord knows how many Gibraltar cases there were. The president of Gibraltar, Mike Lallinger, told me till the day he died, and I suppose he was right, that in all those years I never lost a case for Gibraltar.

I also filed many cases on behalf of Fannin Bank for failure to pay promissory notes and to abide by loan agreements. These cases usually ended in summary judgments for the bank. There were bunches of them.

Some case stories, however, must be told, and on these remaining pages I will try to be choosy.

One of the most interesting cases I tried was *Amerada Hess v. Fluor Corporation*. One day I had a call from Mr. Leon Hess, of Amerada Hess in New York City, asking me to come to New York to discuss handling a case for him on behalf of Amerada against Fluor.

I was very impressed with Mr. Hess and eagerly got into the case. Amerada had built a refinery on St. Croix in the Virgin Islands. The engineering contractor firm on the job was Fluor. This refinery at the time was the largest oil refinery in the world, and Fluor had built this refinery for the benefit of Amerada for about $750 million, which at the time was an astronomical sum.

There was just one problem: it didn't work. In installing the refractory, or insulation, on the interior walls of the large cracking towers, somehow or another salt water had been mixed with the refractory material, and after several days of operation, this monstrous refinery came to a sudden halt.

It was a horrible mess. All of the refractory or insulation fell from the interior of the towers. Not only did it delay Amerada for months and months in producing their product, but it also was going to cost another fortune to repair the faulty work. The shutdown time and the engineering costs created damages of approximately $100 million.

Mr. Hess was insistent that I file the case by Friday. I told him it could be done, that all I had to do was to prepare the pleadings, get his approval, and walk across the street to the federal courthouse in Houston, and we'd be in court.

MEET MR. HESS

He surprised me by saying that this case would not be filed in Houston, but would be filed by me in St. Croix. This prompted me to ask him a question: "Why do you need me for your lawyer? You have New York lawyers; you have Miami lawyers; you have Virgin Islands lawyers. Why don't you use them?"

His answer was, "I like Houston lawyers." He said, "As a matter of fact, two weeks ago I was visiting in Washington, D.C., having dinner with John Connally," who was at that time head of the largest law firm in Texas. He told me he asked Governor Connally if he had a personal lawsuit, that involved him personally, which of his lawyers would he hire to represent him. And Mr. Hess told me that Governor Connally told him without hesitation, "I wouldn't hire any of them. I would hire a lawyer by the name of Joe Reynolds in Houston." And he said, "That's how I picked you out to try this lawsuit for me."

I filed the lawsuit on time and for the next year I spent nearly two weeks a month in the Virgin Islands. I normally stayed at the "Hess Hilton," a Quonset hut at the refinery. But those were Golden Days. I managed to take each member of my family on one or more occasions, all with the blessings of Mr. Hess, and the depositions carried us not only to St. Croix and St. Thomas, but to New York, California, and other interesting places. He told me I had to win the case. It never occurred to me we wouldn't. All the facts and the law were on our side.

Sometime in the month of December, I was in St. Croix picking the jury, in the federal court of St. Croix (a United States island), when the jury selection was interrupted as I received a message that the general counsel of Amerada wanted to speak to me on the phone.

The judge, who by this time was my very close personal friend, invited me to use his chambers. So I went to the phone to talk to the general counsel of Amerada. He told me the case had been settled, and he asked me to convey this information to the judge, as well as the lawyer representing Fluor. He explained that on Saturday, Mr. Hess had been playing golf at Pebble Beach in California, where he just happened to run into Bob Fluor, the president of Fluor Corporation, and they played a round of golf together at Pebble Beach.

As they approached the tee for the 18th hole, either Mr. Hess or Mr. Fluor suggested they settle the case on a high-low basis, which they agreed to do, with the high-low figure being determined by who won the 18th hole. And so in this manner, the case was settled.

I was chagrined, disappointed. The general counsel said, "Well, I promise you we'll get you another case better than this one." Then he said, "Well, don't you want to know whether you won or lost the case?" I said, "Yes, I'd like to know." He said, "You lost." But Mr. Hess kept his promise, and I had the privilege of doing other cases for him in Houston. The president of his company was Mr. Mac McCollum, who had become my friend, and who lived in Houston.

Before leaving my reminiscences about this case, it was during depositions in Wilmington that I received an amazing phone call. Joe Greenhill, Chief Justice of the Supreme Court of Texas at the time of the deposition, interrupted. His message to me was that there was a vacancy on the Supreme Court of Texas, and that Governor [Dolph] Briscoe wanted to appoint me to that vacancy. The next day in Houston the governor called to tell me of the appointment. I just had one problem: we couldn't move to Austin. We just couldn't do it. Dolph suggested that we live at our farm in Brenham. Even that was impossible.

On another occasion Dolph asked me again to take an appointment to the Supreme Court. But I just wanted to be a trial lawyer.

A couple of years ago, Amerada was laying a pipeline under the Houston Ship Channel and hired a contractor to lay the pipeline

MEET MR. HESS

under the channel, which could be done under law, as long as the construction did not interfere with ship traffic in the channel. This meant that these huge 30-inch lines, tripled, had to be 50 feet under the bottom of the channel. You see what's coming. The contractor blew it, and never dug his tunnels to properly install the pipeline. And after the contractor wrecked equipment, railroad tracks, and even the Hess Terminal, Mr. McCollum fired the contractor. Naturally, the contractor sued. I have to tell you about this case.

This was a 1993 case, tried in Judge Scott Link's court, and because I was trying to cut back on my trial schedule, I asked Ed Junell in my office to become lead counsel. The lawyer representing the contractor was a young lawyer by the name of Dick Schwartz. The case involved a lot of money. The contractor claimed he had lost profits on the contract of several million dollars.

But the interesting thing is that before the trial started, a very prominent jury consultant called and asked me if he could act as a jury consultant for Amerada on this case; that he would keep his fee at a minimum, not to exceed a certain figure; and that he wanted to open a Houston office, and this would give him that opportunity. I went to Mr. Mac, who was in his 80s and had retired as president of Amerada, but still ran the Houston office. Mr. Mac said, "Do what you want to do." So I hired this expert to be my jury consultant. And at the time there was nobody better.

As we were exposed to the jury panel, several things happened. First of all, the number one juror sitting on the panel was a young girl 21 years of age. When Dick Schwartz, representing the plaintiff, got up to do his *voir dire* of the panel, after a few minutes of explaining about the case, this young lady raised her hand and asked the judge if she could make a statement, and the nice Judge Link said, "of course."

This young, attractive, blond girl stood up and said, "I cannot be a fair juror in this case. I hate lawyers. I think all lawyers are crooks, and there's no way I could be impartial to any lawyer for either side in this case." And she added, "What's more, I hate judges, and I think this is a waste of time and a mockery, and I don't want to be a part of it."

The judge was stunned; Dick Schwartz was speechless; and we all stood there like a bunch of dum-dums. Finally, I asked the judge if I could say something. He begged me to. So I stood up, and addressing the young lady primarily but the panel as a whole, I said that I had known the plaintiff's lawyer since he was a child; that although he was on the other side of the case from me, his mother and father had been my friends and would always be my friends. I told them that Dick Schwartz was an outstanding lawyer; that he was a person of integrity; that he was an honest man; that he knew what he was doing; that his was not a frivolous case; and that a jury was needed to resolve this problem.

I then turned to Ed Junell, my young partner, and I said, "Likewise, Ed Junell's mother and father have been my friends for many, many years, and I have known Ed since he was a young man, and I can truthfully say that he is a man of integrity, one of the finest lawyers in Houston, and that if she, and the panel, would sit on this case, they could see how the system was supposed to work, and how the judicial system in America had contributed to its greatness."

I then turned to the judge and asked him to comment to the panel and tell the jury if he had ever had a juror, in all his years of being a judge, complain about a case being dull or boring. And the judge with a smile on his face said, "I've never had a juror who didn't enjoy having served on a case."

And I asked again if this panel would help resolve the problem in this time-honored way, as we had inherited it since the Ninth Century of England, and it had lasted for over a thousand years as the greatest system ever devised by man to resolve problems. And then the young lady looked me in the eye and said, "I don't believe a word you said."

MEET MR. HESS

We dismissed her and proceeded to pick the jury, but her words had already inflamed the jurors, and it also had given them a technique for getting off of the jury. So we were down to the bottom of the pile. But as we selected the jury, my jury consultant was at his best. Knowing that picking this jury was going to be limited, we went into the jury room and he told me after my six strikes that some way or another, I had to get that black truck driver off the jury; I had to get that black school teacher off the jury; and I had to get that woman CPA who handled nothing but small clients off that jury.

I hasten to add, both the jury consultant and I agreed that I needed on that jury two lawyers, one of whom worked for a friend of mine, the other who was in a large law firm, and the woman who was the office manager of the Exxon Law Department. Those were the kinds of jurors this jury consultant expert said I had to have. All six of these people ended up on the jury.

After two weeks of trial, the bailiff, my friend, walked up to me and said, "Mr. Reynolds, settle this case." Why she said it, I don't know. But she got my attention. So I approached the judge and said, "Judge, perhaps we should take time and try to settle this case." He recessed the jury until two o'clock, and we proceeded to negotiate back and forth, and we finally came to a figure we would recommend and Dick would recommend. But I had to have the approval of Mr. Mac, who had already been my witness but had gone back to his office to do some work.

So I rushed up to Mr. Mac's office at Amerada, and he listened to my story. We called the general counsel, who was the same general counsel who had called me in St. Croix, and both of them said to me, "Do what you think is best." Then Mr. Mac said an interesting thing. "I will settle this case on these conditions, provided you are given the opportunity to question each juror at the conclusion of the settlement talks, as to what was their attitude about the case."

I called the judge on the phone, told him Mr. Mac had agreed on the terms, and the judge said, "Well, come on back; the jury's just coming back from lunch." So I hastened back to the courthouse, and as I walked in the courtroom, the jury clapped and cheered for me. I presumed the judge had told them I had gone to see Mr. Mac, the 80-year-old witness they had heard testify several days before.

Following the announcement of settlement, and consistent with what the court had told me I could do and with what Mr. Mac asked me to do, under my jury consultant's studious vigil, I questioned first the lawyer/juror who worked for my friend. He said, "Mr. Reynolds, I was going to vote against you. I think Amerada is a huge American company, and I think they should have given this little Houston contractor a second bite at the apple. So I was ready to rule against you." I was chagrined and shocked.

I turned to the second lawyer/juror, who worked for the large firm. He said, "Mr. Reynolds, I think your people were too technical. They held that young contractor to too tight a standard. I would have ruled against you." I turned to the Exxon lady, and she said, "I hated everything about your side." My three choices for jurors had all been against me!

But at this time the black truck driver, whom the jury consultant had told me I had to strike, said, "Mr. Reynolds, may I ask you a question?"

I said, "Yes."

He said, "Did Mr. Mac testify that he was 83 years old?"

I said, "Yes."

He said, "Did Mr. Mac testify that he never graduated from high school?"

I said, "Yes."

MEET MR. HESS

And he said, "And yet he became president of Amerada Hess, one of the biggest corporations in America?"

I said, "Yes."

And this black truck driver turned to the rest of the jury and said, "See, I told you that's what he said." And then he turned to me and he said "Mr. Reynolds, I wish you would tell Mr. Mac for me that I think he's the kind of person that made America great. And I respect him as much as any man I've ever seen or met."

The black school teacher said, "Mr. Reynolds, didn't you used to be the attorney for North Forest School District?" I said, "Yes." She said, "I remember all the things you did for all the little children out at North Forest, and I couldn't wait to rule in your favor."

And then the lady CPA, whom the jury consultant had told me to strike at all costs, asked me a question, and this was it: She said, "Mr. Reynolds, do you have a double?"

I said, "Yes."

She said, "What's his name?"

I said, "Cary Grant."

She laughed and said, "You remind me of my daddy so much. You look just like him; you act just like him; and I believe somewhere back yonder we're from the same family."

The point of this long story is to publish loud and clear that the jury consultants of this world and the Joe Reynoldses of this world can never tell you what a jury is going to do.

I like juries. And I used to have a sign above my office door that said that lawyers who would not try their cases to juries were cowards. One day Joe Jamail came by my office and told me he was making a speech out at the University of Houston law school, and could he take that sign with him? I told him he could, and I never saw it again.

No one can predict juries. And if I've tried 400 lawsuits, I would always pick a jury over a judge. Because until recent years, juries have not been political. Much publicity has made them political, and that's why publicity and the media interfering with the trying of lawsuits brings politics into the courtroom and dismantles the jury system. And this should not be.

Leave the jury alone, and in nearly every case, it will come up with the right decision.

One other Hess story. One Sunday afternoon Mr. Hess called me on the phone. He said, "Are you busy?"

I said, "No." He said, "Are you watching the football game?"

I said, "Yes,"

He said, "How would you like to be coach of the New York Jets?"

I was just about to interrupt him, but my mouth was frozen.

He said, " I just fired the Jets coach, Weeb Eubank, and I just traded Joe Namath. I'm looking for somebody who knows nothing about football. Are you available? You can still be my lawyer."

And that was Mr. Hess. I'm glad you got to meet him.

CHAPTER **12**

10b-5

Starting in the early 1970s, I became involved in a relatively new field of federal litigation known as "10b-5," which is a regulation of the Securities and Exchange Commission, section 10(b)(5). This simply pertains to civil fraud resulting from the buying and selling of corporate stock in interstate commerce. There has to be a buyer and there has to be a seller. Lawyers call these cases "ten-bee-five" cases.

My first involvement began with my representation of a growth Texas life insurance company that sold its stock and investments to another life insurance company in Alabama. The lawsuit alleged that my client, in selling its stock and securities, failed to disclose certain bad investments owned by my client.

My case was tried in federal court in Birmingham, Alabama, to an Alabama jury. The plaintiff was represented by Alabama lawyers claiming to be the most experienced and greatest 10b-5 lawyers in America. It was, I think, the first 10b-5 jury case tried in America.

There were multiple defendants and many lawyers, and I headed up the defendants' side of the case. The case was significant to me for several reasons. First, the case started to trial before the jury on January 2, 1972, and the jury reached its verdict in June of 1972. I was in Birmingham continuously for six months, but I came home every weekend on Friday night and returned on Sunday. Among the interesting lawyers was a plaintiff lawyer named Crook and a defendant lawyer named Love. The jury actually rendered its verdict based on those two words! Love won out, which means we won, and Crook lost.

This case was also significant because it led to my involvement in another 10b-5 case in Houston called the Westec debacle. In the criminal side of Westec, I represented a great but naive man who, together with his associate Mr. Williams, had started Westec. The company's stock price increased like crazy.

The stock crashed when it was discovered that my client, not knowing it was illegal, supported the price of Westec's stock and caused its market price to soar by his borrowing large sums of money from T. J. Bettis Company and its president, Mr. John Austin, and Mr. David C. Bintliff, one of Houston's most powerful men. My client went to prison. Then began all of the many civil lawsuits.

At the suggestion of Judge Hannay, I was hired to represent a Chicago corporation, Chemetron, which had traded one of its subsidiary companies to Westec for Westec stock. When the bubble burst, Chemetron had lost $9 million. The case was tried to a jury here in Houston, before Judge Carl Bue. It, too, was a long trial. It was during this trial that I had an interesting experience with a New York stockbroker who graduated from Yale. Here is that story.

He was my expert witness in a trial, and after I presented him on direct examination, my opponent asked, "You're a graduate of Yale, are you, sir?" My witness said, "Yes."

My opponent then produced a piece of paper and asked my witness if he wasn't in fact in the bottom ten percent of his freshman class. My witness said "yes."

I had not seen this alleged transcript and objected to his use of it. After some argument-despite the fact that on it was boldly emblazoned that it was the private property of my witness and not to be used for any purpose-the judge let it in.

My opponent proceeded to ask my expert witness if he wasn't in the bottom 20 percent of his sophomore and junior class and didn't he, indeed, graduate in the bottom 25 percent of his class? My witness answered "yes." My opponent then sat down, after strutting smugly to his seat.

I had no idea what to ask, but I knew something had to be wrong. I asked my witness if he had worked during college. "Yes, I worked my way entirely through Yale," he replied.

I asked what happened to make his grades so low. He said that his first job as a freshman at Yale was with the Coca-Cola Bottling Company and while he was working the line, some of the bottles exploded, hit his eyes, and he went through Yale blind! Needless to say, the effect my opponent thought his cross-examination would have on the jury was not to be.

The jury awarded my client $9 million in actual damages and $9 million in punitive damages, plus interest. However, I made a huge mistake at the conclusion of this trial, which is worth recounting as a reminder for future lawyers not to make that same error.

In federal court, the charge to the jury is made after oral argument, at the conclusion of the case. After argument, the attorneys make oral objections to the charge of the Court, which also follows jury argument. After my long argument in Westec, and after the charge was read to the jury, I was totally exhausted. It was late in the evening, and I made the error of suggesting that the attorneys agree to file written objections to the charge a week later.

Judge Bue agreed to this procedure, but insisted that he wanted to know in substance the nature of our objections, so that he could correct the charge if he felt it was necessary. We made perfunctory objections and we left the courthouse late at night.

A week later, after the jury had rendered its verdict in my favor, the defendants filed their written objections to the charge, after having them prepared by a battery of law professors and attorneys all across America. Both Judge Bue and I had been had. It was my error. The Fifth Circuit blasted my charge, and I was looking at the real possibility of having to try this case again over the next six months.

We appealed the Fifth Circuit's ruling to the United States Supreme Court, and the Supreme Court vacated the Fifth Circuit's opinion.

During the appellate process, we settled this case by having Chemetron accept approximately two-thirds of the jury award.

But there is another story from this case, having to do with the people, not the law, that is worth recounting. The jury had found that the Bettis company, together with its president, Mr. John Austin, and David C. Bintliff and Arthur Andersen were all guilty of a civil conspiracy to defraud my client, Chemetron. Mr. Bintliff seemed to have financed the building of Houston. Both Mr. Bintliff and Mr. Austin were two major pillars of Houston. Bettis Company was Houston's biggest mortgage company at the time.

Years later, I was asked to be the master of ceremonies at the honoring of Mr. Gibson Gayle, my friend, when he was named the Lawyer of the Year in Houston. Mr. Bintliff shared the podium with me as the spokesman for the Baylor Medical Schools honoring Mr. Gayle. I had to introduce Mr. Bintliff. Seeing the situation, I walked over to Mr. Bintliff, held out my hand to him, and said sincerely to this old man, "Mr. Bintliff, I respect you very much, and I want to thank you personally for helping make Houston the great city that it is, and for personally speaking in behalf of my dear friend, Gibson Gayle."

He started crying-Gayle was standing beside me, not even beginning to understand what was going on. Mr. Bintliff very quietly said to me, "Joe, are you sincere and serious?" I said, "Yes."

With that he hugged my neck, sobbed very loudly, and said to me, "You have just given me back my good name. God has answered my prayer. For lo these many years I have prayed for your respect. Now the rest of my life I can live in peace."

We became fast friends. Once a week he'd call. We often ate lunch. We never discussed Westec, but he and I both knew that all was forgiven.

There were many other 10b-5 cases-many for small insurance companies, many from others, including my friend Calvin Guest. And I represented Tenneco in another 10b-5 case, and I represented Judge Ed Coulson before Judge Weinstein in federal court in New York City.

Several years ago, Susie and I were in Williamsburg, Virginia. I noticed at the lodge that a legal seminar was being held by the American Bar Association on 10b-5. On the spur of the moment, I decided to walk in and listen.

I sat down in the auditorium close to the front, just as the expert attorney-lecturer was being introduced. The introducer referred to the speaker as the foremost 10b-5 lawyer in America. And lo and behold, he was the plaintiff's lawyer I had beaten in my Alabama case [name withheld].

As the attending lawyers applauded this expert, he spotted me. His eyes widened, he stood silent for what seemed to be five minutes, then he started coughing. He spoke to the introducer and left the auditorium. The introducer said the seminar speaker had become ill. The meeting adjourned. I rejoined Susie, and we walked over to the Duke of Gloucester Street. I never saw that lawyer again. It's funny how things work out sometimes.

CHAPTER **13**

Joe Jamail

The story of my legal career would not be complete without describing the role that Joe Jamail and Dahr Jamail (one of Joe's fine sons) have played. Time does not permit the whole truth, but at least I need to tell "Nothing But the Truth."

Joe and I had been in the Marine Corps together. I met Joe during the war in George Cire's hospital room at Aiea Heights, Honolulu. Joe was on his way to Guam.

Today Joe is one of the great lawyers of the world. He won the biggest jury verdict in history for Pennzoil against Texaco, $11 Billion.

I was in on the fringes of that great case. About three weeks before the trial date, Dick Miller, attorney for Texaco, filed a motion to disqualify the Baker & Botts lawyers who were acting as Joe's co-counsel, because the Baker & Botts lawyers had represented Pennzoil in the negotiations between Pennzoil and Getty Oil, a key figure in the case. Miller's tactics were to name all of the Baker & Botts attorneys in the case as witnesses, thereby disqualifying them from participating as attorneys in the case. Joe hired me to represent Baker & Botts.

To win, it was necessary to take each lawyer through the Getty negotiations to expose Miller's ploy. It didn't hurt that a few months before, Miller-who had been employed by Baker & Botts-left Baker & Botts, and he had gotten Texaco to waive his representation of his clients in other cases against Texaco and to waive his prior representation of Pennzoil. So we won that skirmish.

We also had to defend the attack upon Judge Sol Casseb, whose qualifications to sit in the case were being challenged. We were also successful in defense of that tactic, which in my opinion was another delay in the trial of the real issues. As a matter of fact, all of these maneuvers were won by us at the trial, court of appeals, and supreme court levels. These proceedings were done on a fast track that was accomplished in a matter of weeks.

The case then proceeded to trial before the jury. It lasted for many weeks. One day, around noon, Dahr called excitedly from the courthouse and shouted that the jury had given Pennzoil an $11 billion-dollar verdict, and that Joe had asked that I meet him in his office in an hour. I called Gibson Gayle and told him the news, and he was thrilled. He said that he was on his way, so I started for Joe's office. On the way over, I ran into Wayne Fisher and invited him to Joe's office. Fisher and I arrived first, Gayle in 30 minutes, and then Joe. The excitement was electric. We laughed, we cried, and we relished every minute.

After an hour or so, the world was looking for Joe and wanted to break down his doors. So Fisher, Gayle, and I started to leave. As we were leaving, Joe called, "Come back!" And the three of us went back to his office. Very pensively, Joe slowly said, "Before this day is over, all three of you will be offered employment to represent Texaco." I interrupted to say, "Joe, Texaco doesn't have enough money left to pay me, and if they did, I wouldn't take it."

I got back to my office and Carol told me that my friend Dempsey Prappas was ringing the phone off the wall, and that he had some kind of an emergency. I went straight to the phone and called this long-time lawyer friend of mine, wondering what had happened to him. Dempsey said, "Joe, I've got you the biggest case in history." He said, "My college roommate at Delaware called me, and he is General Counsel for Texaco. He said he wanted me to hire for him the best lawyer in Houston. I want to hire you. Will you take over the Pennzoil case for Texaco?" I told Dempsey I was very honored, but that there was no way.

Dempsey asked if I had a conflict with either Texaco or Pennzoil, and I said no. He said, "You've got to do it. This is the opportunity of a lifetime. You've got to do it." I told Dempsey, "Maybe next time."

I hung up and called Denice, Jamail's secretary. Joe was being interviewed by the media from all over the world. I told Denice I had to talk to him. Joe came on the phone and I told him, "Old Buddy, you were right. I just turned down Texaco's offer to employ me in the Pennzoil case." Joe called Texaco a dirty name as we hung up.

On the appellate stage, Joe had me represent the largest stockholders of Pennzoil, so I continued to be involved.

Finally, after the court of appeals had ruled in Joe's favor on the merits of the case, Joe and I were trying to anticipate what the Texas Supreme Court would do. Joe was pessimistic and said that the Supreme Court had to take the case. I said, "no way." I told him that the court of appeals opinion was great, and besides, "the Supreme Court doesn't want this hot potato." We talked and talked and talked. Finally I said to Joe, "You have a brand new Jaguar. I have an old Cadillac. I'll bet my car against your car that the Supreme Court says no to the writ." Joe said, "You've got it."

The very next day, Joe called. "You won my car. The Supreme Court turned down the writ." I said, "deliver my Jaguar to my house."

The next day, Susie called me in great distress. I couldn't get off of another call. She persisted. I finally got off the phone and she said, "There is a wrecker out in our driveway, pulling a broken-down, wrecked hearse. She asked what she should do with it and then said, "wait a minute." She was gone about five minutes and finally returned, to tell me she had just paid the wrecker driver $50 to carry the wrecked hearse to Clyde Wilson's house.

That night I learned that Clyde's wife had called him in tears, and that Clyde had made a lucky guess and had paid the wrecker driver $100 to haul the wrecked hearse to Joe Jamail's beach house in Galveston. What goes around, comes around.

Pennzoil was over, but not the story. Six years later, Jamail was beating up on Coopers & Lybrand in a 10b-5 case in Galveston. I was in the middle of a deposition in California in the *Western Waste* case. I was questioning the witness. My deposition was interrupted by Joe Jamail telling me the jury had just returned a verdict for his client of $600 million! I was very happy for him.

Fifteen minutes later I had another interruption. Dempsey Prappas was calling. Dempsey had another emergency. He told me his next-door neighbor was the head of Coopers & Lybrand, and at Dempsey's suggestion, Coopers & Lybrand was hiring Joe Reynolds to take over the case.

Then Dempsey added, "You told me last time that the next time you would do it. This is the next time."

I told Dempsey, "I can't do it." He begged, and said, "why not? Why not? What's Jamail got on you?"

I said, "Joe has nothing on me." I said, "Dempsey, Joe is my Marine Corps buddy."

I then called Joe from Los Angeles. I said, "Guess what just happened?"

He said, "Don't tell me Dempsey Prappas called you and that he has another roommate!" I said, "No, this time it was his next-door neighbor, who heads up Coopers & Lybrand." Joe said something that sounded like "Semper Fi," and he and I both laughed.

Don't get the idea that Joe's and my relationship worked only one way. Joe and Dahr have done many great things for me. Many times, they have helped me, brought me business, and contributed toward my retirement.

Then there was the famous *Keck* case. Joe, Dahr, Fisher, Bill Miller, and I represented one side of the Keck family. The same Dick Miller, Jack McConn, Tom Alexander, and Franci Beck represented the other side of the Keck family.

This battle was a family feud over the division of proceeds of the sale of Pure Oil Company to Arco. We were taking a deposition in Joe's office of Mr. Keck, Miller's client. Joe started the deposition by asking Mr. Keck, "State your name."

Miller interrupted and said he would not answer that question. "You know this man's name. Go to the next question." Joe yelled something at Miller. Miller yelled something back. Alexander screamed at me. Fisher ran over to the corner of the room. I told Alexander to sit down.

Miller turned on me and said, "Step out of this room, and I'm going to whip your *#!!." Dahr Jamail, with all of his 120 pounds, rushed at Miller, shouting, "You'll have to whip me first." Miller and I stepped outside the room and Dahr rushed in between us, screaming at Miller, "This is my fight, and you don't have the guts to fight."

Fisher banged on the table, and peace was restored. The deposition ended, then and there. The next day, Judge Solito put the deposition under lock and key over my protest. I begged the judge for the right to send a copy to each law school in Texas, to teach future lawyers how *not* to take a deposition.

Somewhere during these same years, Ed Junell and I had been prosecuting an antitrust case against Toyota, claiming that they were exercising and illegal tying arrangement. "Tying" is an illegal condition of selling a product. For example, "We'll sell you X if you buy X and Y." The sale of X is tied to the sale of Y. It's against the law.

Another example of an illegal tying arrangement that violates the antitrust laws happens when a bank lends money to buy a property, conditioned upon the borrower's buying a second piece of property at the same time from the same lender. Banks have done this to unload foreclosed properties that they couldn't otherwise sell.

In the *Toyota* case, in order to buy their Toyota automobiles, you had to buy all of their accessories as well. Such practices, for example, eliminated RCA from selling radios for Toyota automobiles. The same would apply to other accessories, such as air conditioners. Toyota would install their own products and prevent the buyer from getting products from the seller of their choice.

A&P was also found to have violated the antitrust laws by tying the sale of a certain brand of peas, for example, or to the purchase of vinegar or some other product unwanted by the purchaser. Usually this second product would have a marked-up price. This eventually led to a perfectly legal practice we see today, which is of a grocery store carrying its own label on certain products.

We settled the *Toyota* case in my office, and as we were signing the final papers, Mr. Galloway, the Regional Vice President for

Toyota, said, "there is one thing left to say." He stated, "Joe, I am giving you a Toyota car, but it's on the condition that you never sue Toyota again." I was surprised at this, but I told Mr. Galloway he could take his Toyota and shove it. Mr. Galloway was offended and hurt. He thought he was doing something very nice for me, and in truth, he was. But I wouldn't take his Toyota.

A few months later, on Christmas morning, I walked out of my front door and there was a brand-new Chevrolet car sitting in my driveway, with a note that said, "Merry Christmas from Barry Galloway." He really wanted me to have this car.

I gave the Chevrolet to my former daughter-in-law Nancy. A few days later, Mr. Galloway called and was concerned that I had given away his gift. A few days later still, he came by my house and delivered to me a Toyota Celica, telling me that this was not Toyota's car, but his wife's car, and that they had to get rid of it, so it was a gift to me. He explained that I had to keep it for my own use. And because he was such a nice fellow, I became the owner of a Toyota car.

The next day, I drove my new Toyota downtown, zipping in and out of traffic, using that 5-speed transmission on the floor. When I got to my office, I received a call from Joe Jamail, who told me he had just received a call from my wife, who was very hurt that I would drive a Toyota. Then Jamail said, "Remember Pearl Harbor."

This conversation was followed up by a hand-delivered note from Joe and Dahr, stating, "Remember Pearl Harbor." That night I gave the car back to Barry Galloway.

Several years ago, Tom Cordell and I were representing Eugene Cook and his law firm in Marsha Anthony's court. When we arrived in her courtroom, the courtroom was full of lawyers appearing there that morning on docket call. Judge Anthony stated, "Mr. Reynolds has just come into the courtroom, and before we proceed, I am going to have him tell the famous Joe Jamail story." Here it is.

I had been sick with hepatitis, which I got from eating shrimp in Amsterdam. I had been out of the office for a number of months, barely able to lift my head off the pillow. It's a horrible illness.

I had returned to try a Gibraltar case in Tom Stovall's court. At the first recess, the bailiff in Judge Reagan Cartwright's court came around and asked me to come to Judge Cartwright's court, where Mr. Jamail was trying a case.

I walked into the courtroom, and the lawyer opposite Mr. Jamail was cross-examining the witness. The jury was very attentive. Jamail's head was folded on his arms. As I walked within the rail, Jimmie Lee Rusk, the beautiful court reporter, stood up, threw down her pen, rushed up to me, threw her arms around my neck, and kissed me on the lips! The jury gasped-as did I-and Judge Cartwright choked.

Finally, Judge Cartwright cleared his throat and told the jury, "This is Mr. Joe Reynolds. He's been very sick. He is my favorite lawyer. I think he's the best lawyer that's ever been in my courtroom. Besides, he is a Christian gentleman."

Then he asked me, "Joe, what are you doing in my courtroom?" And before I could answer, Jamail jumped up and stated, without any hesitation, "Your Honor, Mr. Reynolds is my co-counsel. Joe, have a seat right here next to me."

The judge glared. Opposing counsel leaped to his feet, and the judge told the bailiff, "Take the jury out." The case settled in the next 30 minutes.

Another Jamail story I have told many times involves a case where we were on opposite sides in the courtroom. It was a bill of review case in a divorce, and Joe represented Percy Foreman, while I represented Red McCombs, who at the time of this writing is the owner of the San Antonio Spurs. (See the "Legal Leftovers" chapter for more about this case.)

During that final arguments of that case, Jamail told the jury that I may have been a fine marine, but that I was a "p___-poor lawyer." When I got up for my final argument, I told the jury that Jamail wasn't even a good marine! We had fun, and my client won that case.

The Jamail stories are endless, but they represent some of the richest experiences of my life.

Joe's beautiful wife and lifetime love Lee passed away recently, after a battle with cancer. It was a sad time for all of us, and I couldn't help but wonder what a wreck I would be if I ever lost my sweet Susie.

Jamail still goes to his office every day, because-well, that's what we lawyers do.

CHAPTER **14**

Lawsuits and More Lawsuits

THE DOMED STADIUM

The longest case I ever tried involved and is still called "The Domed Stadium Case." In the '60s, Harris County built a domed stadium, and it was nicknamed "The 8th Wonder of the World." It cost a whopping $30 million.

The roof was glass, so as to allow sunlight onto the playing field, to enable grass to grow. The only problem with this design was that temperature variations between night and day caused the glass to contract and expand daily, thereby creating gaps in the roof. And so it rained as if there were no roof.

The problem was so severe that when I would go to a football game, I took my umbrella to every game in this indoor stadium, 8th Wonder of the World. It was that bad. The grass died. The roof leaked. And the air conditioning never worked. In the fall of the year, it would be so foggy inside the Dome, you might as well be listening to a ball game on the radio. You couldn't see much.

As you can expect, everyone was sued. Again, many of the top famous lawyers were involved in this case: Tom Phillips of the state antitrust case reported earlier in this book, represented the Houston Sports Association, the plaintiff.

Ben Sewell and Preston Shirley represented the two architectural firms.

Jim Winters represented a contractor; A. J. Watkins represented the glass company; and Frank Bean represented another contractor.

I represented U.S. Steel, fabricator of the steel used in the roof.

A few weeks into the case, it became apparent that this case would never end, and the judge, Judge Bill Blanton, talked all of us into waiving the jury. This was a godsend. It gave us flexibility in our schedules and enabled us to carry on a law practice, despite the ongoing nature of this lawsuit.

Our defense was facetious; we claimed the roof didn't leak. Well, that's not true. Our defense really was that we could not be held responsible because our design and the fabrication of the roof support did not cause the problem. But it's not the issues of the case that make it so important. The significance of the case has to do with its uniqueness.

The lawyers were great, the judge was great, but during the course of this trial, more discovery of evidence became necessary. After several weeks of trial, the court ordered inspection and depositions concerning the condition of the interior and the exterior of the dome roof. Remember, the height of the dome was several hundred feet, probably the height of a 20-story building.

I didn't like heights, but I was lucky. My young partner, Bucky Cunningham, was a great athlete. I'm serious. He was a Little All-American split end at William & Mary. He even tried out for the

LAWSUITS AND MORE LAWSUITS

Washington Redskins. He was and is a great tennis player and could easily have made a living as a pro golfer.

But what made Bucky a natural to this case was that he would rush in where angels feared to tread. He couldn't wait to inspect the roof himself! They actually took depositions on top of the dome during the case.

The old lawyers complained to me, because Bucky kept pushing them to the upper limits. They walked the cat roof, which hardly is visible from the seats in the dome. Bucky intimidated the other lawyers with his agility and daring. Meanwhile, I was back at the office.

It is because of the length and the general community interest in this case that I include it, but there is another reason, and this is the real one. By the time of the trial, my friend and distinguished lawyer for the plaintiff, Tom Phillips, who was head of the Baker & Botts trial section, had grown old. He had been one of the great trial lawyers of Texas. But at this stage of his career, his memory was not good, he forgot people's names, and he continually misplaced documents. They tell me this is the sign that a trial lawyer is over the hill. (Now, where did I put the rest of my notes about this case?)

It was then and there that I made a pledge to myself to quit before I became forgetful and inadequate. Somewhere along the way to the courthouse, I forgot my pledge, I think.

At the end of a five-month trial, I felt older than Tom Phillips, but I was rejuvenated when the judge ruled in our favor. And the whole world now has "Astroturf" where grass won't grow.

As I write this, the Astrodome still stands, but now the Houston Astros play their baseball games in the new Minute Maid Park in downtown Houston, and the Houston Texans play football in Reliant Stadium, just across the way from the Dome. Another era ends and yet another begins.

Turning from baseball to football, I remember a story about the Dallas Cowboys. In the '80s, my friend Ed Smith of Houston owned 28 percent of the Cowboys franchise. He liked owning an interest in the Cowboys, and it brought him a lot of pleasure. And he was interested in maintaining that interest.

One of his co-owners was Mr. Bum Bright, with whom I had served on the Board of Regents at Texas A&M. Bum owned 40 percent of the Cowboys franchise. Bum owned 100 percent of the lease of the Texas Stadium, where the Cowboys played football. It was a beautiful working arrangement, and the Cowboys were successful. But hard times came to Bum. Bum was in the oil business, and in 1986 the oil business, which had built Texas, went into a deep depression, and Bum and many other Texans lost their proverbial shirts. Bum had to sell his interest in the Cowboys.

He approached Ed, and Ed agreed to purchase, from his friend Bum, Bum's 100 percent interest in Texas Stadium and Bum's 40 percent in the Cowboys. The arrangement was that Ed would pay Bum $40 million for his interest in Texas Stadium and purchase Bum's interest in the Cowboy franchise on the basis of evaluating the franchise at $80 million. They shook hands.

So Ed started making arrangements to get his financing. He had it all in place; the papers were drawn; and then Ed learned *from the media* that Bum had been offered a better deal by a man named Jerry Jones from Arkansas. We learned from Tom Landry, the coach of the Cowboys, and others, that Jerry Jones approached Bum and told Bum he would like to buy Bum's interest in the Cowboys and the Stadium, and Bum explained to Jerry Jones that he had already made a deal with Ed Smith.

LAWSUITS AND MORE LAWSUITS

Jones asked Bum, "Well what kind of a deal did you make with Ed Smith, if you don't mind telling me?" Bum explained the deal, and as he finished, Jerry Jones said to Bum, "I'll make you a better deal. I will buy your 100 percent interest in Texas Stadium for $80 million, and I will buy your interest in the Cowboy franchise on the basis of it being valued at $40 million."

Bum couldn't turn down the offer, but he was smart enough to require Jerry Jones, as a condition to the deal, to indemnify him against any claims or lawsuits that Ed Smith might bring. And Jones had his lawyer prepare that indemnity.

Ed was crushed. Jones took over. He fired Tom Landry. Dallas was ready to lynch Jones, and Ed approached me. We prepared a lawsuit against Jones for tortious interference of Ed's contract with Bum.

And then we met with Bum's lawyer and Jones's lawyer. As they pooh-poohed our case, I told them both to go read the *Pennzoil* case (referred to earlier in these memoirs), that the execution of the indemnity from Jones to Bum was *prima facie* evidence of tortious interference with the contract or the anticipated agreement between Bum on the one hand and Ed on the other. Almost at the courthouse steps, Jones cratered and paid Ed his rightful amount for his 28 percent ownership of the Cowboys.

Jerry Jones did not like me. In fact, that is an understatement. But in my business, history seems to repeat itself. As in my *Toyota* case, at the settlement conference, Jerry Jones said that he had a gift for me. And it was two season tickets for the Cowboy games at Texas Stadium, but that I wouldn't like the tickets, because he was placing me right behind the goalpost, where I couldn't see a thing.

Later, and after the lawsuit was over, and as we write this narrative, the Cowboy franchise has become the most valuable professional franchise of any sport in America, and Ed Smith has now decided, after the passing of time, that Reynolds *lost* his case.

CLIENTS WHO PAID THE OVERHEAD

How do lawyers get clients? It's hard to say. My experience may be different from other lawyers', and I don't know the answer to this question. All I know is that for most of my career as a lawyer, it was my friends who opened doors for me. It was my clients who became my friends and vice-versa, and that enabled me eventually to build a law firm of more than a hundred lawyers.

Over the years I was fortunate enough to be the trial lawyer for many financial institutions in Houston. For example, Harold Jones, a banker, a client, and a friend, gave me the privilege of representing Fannin Bank during the '50s, '60s, and '70s. Fannin Bank was a middle-sized bank in a fast-growing area, and it was a fast-growing bank. I was given the privilege of handling all of the outside trial work and filing suits for collection of notes, enforcing loan agreements, and generally serving as the bank's trial counsel.

Through another friend, I became outside trial counsel for Republic Savings of Texas, which until the mid-'80s was one of the leading savings and loans in Texas. In addition, I was privileged to represent Continental Bank & Trust, which later became Allied Bank (later still, it became First Interstate Bank, and ultimately it was merged into Wells Fargo Bank). The principals of this bank were friends of mine, and I represented the principals in individual cases, and through those relationships I became outside trial counsel for the bank. For the purposes of this record, I want to name those good friends.

One of those principals was Mr. Walter Mischer Sr., one of the leading movers and shakers of Houston. He was an outstanding

LAWSUITS AND MORE LAWSUITS

man and when he passed away in December 2005 at the age of 83 it was a great loss to many people and organizations. He helped build our city.

The Executive Vice President, and later the CEO, of the bank was Mr. Gerald Smith, who was a very gifted banker and an interesting individual, who is still my friend. Mr. Mike Wells was the Operating Officer of the bank, and I dealt with him on a very frequent basis. Mike and I served with the Horse Committee of the Houston Livestock Show & Rodeo for many years, and he was also one of Mr. Freeman's boys. Finally, the Chairman of the Board of that bank was Mr. Jack Trotter, a friend and a personal client. Allied Bank used many lawyers from our firm, and our firm did much business with that bank. It was a great client and a great bank.

But the main focus of my attention in talking about representing financial institutions must be on Gibraltar Savings & Loan. Gibraltar was the largest savings and loan in Texas, and it had as its president a man by the name of Mike Lallinger. Mike Lallinger was a gifted banker, and he was the chief operating person of this mammoth savings and loan. I met Mr. Lallinger under very interesting circumstances.

In 1965, Susie's friend Helen Walker, who lived at the corner of Voss and Memorial, called me and said that she and her family were going to sell their home at that corner of Voss and Memorial, and that she thought we should buy it. She explained that since Dan had a horse, which he kept at their place, we should just buy their home. She told me that Susie loved their house and she would love living there. The only problem I could see was that I didn't know how we could pay for it.

The Walker home at Voss & Memorial consisted of about six and a half acres, and it was more than we could afford. However, I mentioned it to Susie, and she, of course, liked the house. But still, it was impossible for us. Or so I thought. I keep learning that God has other plans for us sometime.

The very next day I went across the hall and was visiting with my client and friend, Sterling Hogan, who is one of the great men I have known in my life. I mentioned this to Sterling, and Sterling said, "Well you have to buy it. There's no way you cannot buy that place. The price she has given you is a very fair price, and you have to buy the place." And without asking my permission, he called to his secretary, Mrs. Guinn, and said, "Mrs. Guinn, get Mike Lallinger on the phone." I had never heard of Mike Lallinger until that moment.

Shortly, Mr. Hogan was on the phone talking to "Mike." And he told Mike that he had a friend, a lawyer named Joe Reynolds, who was sitting in his office, who had an opportunity to buy six and a half acres at Voss and Memorial Drive, and that he, Mr. Hogan, wanted Gibraltar to make me a loan for 100 percent of the purchase price, and that he was sending me to see Mr. Lallinger.

At the close of that conversation with Mike, Sterling Hogan turned to me and said, "I've arranged for you to meet with Mike Lallinger in an hour."

I said, "Well, Sterling, there's no way I can pay for that," and Sterling said, "I think there is." Sterling said, "I'll tell you what we'll do. We'll subdivide the front portion of the property. You can create five lots by putting a road down the middle. You will then sell those lots and that will pay for your property." He said, "as a matter of fact, since I have nothing better to do, and since I've been a developer all my life, I will do this just to give me something to do, and in that way, you can afford to buy the property. You will have the house, you will have a place to keep the horses, and it will be a wonderful place to live."

LAWSUITS AND MORE LAWSUITS

With that, he called out again to Mrs. Guinn and said, "Call George Reed." They then had a short conversation about doing a survey and platting a street there in this property that he insisted that I buy.

I left Sterling's office not knowing what to do, but I did go to see Mr. Lallinger. Mr. Lallinger was very friendly, and I was impressed. He told me that he had checked me out, and that he would make the loan. He said, "I will lend you 100 percent of the purchase price, and as I understand it, you're going to develop the property, so there will no problem in paying back Gibraltar."

Somehow or another I got out of his office and went home and talked to Susie about it. I signed the earnest money contract, and we were in the process of buying the Walker house at Voss and Memorial. Before the closing, Susie and I spent sleepless nights wondering how we'd pay for it. We loved our home on Lynbrook. It was a modest home that we could afford, and buying this other property represented a very huge investment. We were *very* concerned.

After we had signed the earnest money contract and before the closing, I got a call from Mike Lallinger. It scared me to death. I imagined everything in the world. I figured he had changed his mind, that he was not going to let us have the money, and there would be no closing. I thought, "well, maybe that's the best thing for us."

In any event, I drove out to Mike's office and went in to his office there at Gibraltar Savings Bank, and he met me and was very friendly. He said, "Come on in, I want to talk to you." I knew that it was going to be bad news. As I sat down there in his office, Mike looked at me and said, "I'm not going to let you subdivide that property."

I said, "But Mike, I *have* to! There's no other way." He said, "No." He said, "that property is going to be your home." He said, "I am not going to let you subdivide it. You will live there, and you and Susie will make your home there, and it will be your *residence*, where you *live*. And you will be happy there. But it would be criminal for you to subdivide it. That property all goes together."

I again protested. I said, "Mike, I'm worried about how I'm going to pay for it." He said, "Well, quit worrying. I have the solution."

I said, "Well, I'd sure like to hear it, because I am worried."

He said, "Well, here is the solution. You have just become the trial lawyer for Gibraltar." He said, "We will furnish you enough business that will keep you in legal business in Houston as long as you care to be a lawyer." He said, "My next-door neighbor is one of your friends, and my next-door neighbor tells me that you are the greatest lawyer in the world."

He went on: "You have a friend by the name of Platt Turner, and Platt Turner says that you've been his lawyer, that you represent him now, that you are a great Christian individual, and that there is no better lawyer than Joe Reynolds."

Mike said again, "You've just become Gibraltar's lawyer." He said, "We have lots of business, and moreover, we never settle cases, because if we settle them, then we get hit by all kinds of frivolous cases. So when someone sues Gibraltar, we have to take it to trial." He said, "You will now have enough legal business to keep you from worrying about this purchase, and we will keep you busy for the rest of your life."

We bought the property at Voss and Memorial, and for the next 25 years, I handled nearly all of Gibraltar's cases. Mike Lallinger became my friend. Mike Lallinger had been introduced to me by

LAWSUITS AND MORE LAWSUITS

two of my other great friends, Sterling Hogan and Platt Turner. And without these friends, none of this would have happened.

After getting this news, I went straight to Sterling's office, and I told him what Mike had said, and he laughed and said, "Well, you've just taken away from me the only job I had!" He said, "I'm sorry you're not going to subdivide it, but I am in complete agreement with Mike."

A few years ago I was visiting with Mike, and Mike was laughing and smiling, and he said, "You know something? In 25 years of your being the lawyer for Gibraltar, you never lost a case." I hadn't thought of it, but I did remind him: "Well, I may not have lost any for Gibraltar, but I did lose some others."

Some of my losses came during the '80s, a turbulent time for Houston's economy, and Kay Morgan and Charles Peterson had the misfortune of working with me on many of them. I don't know what I would have done without them.

No trial lawyer can ever claim 100 percent victories, unless he or she just doesn't try very many cases and has the luxury of being very selective.

But I always enjoyed representing my friends, and in most cases, if we weren't friends before the case started, we were when it was over.

Without friends who know you and love you, success is hard to come by.

CHAPTER 15

Winding Down

Toward the end of my active career, two cases stand out among the rest: *Texas Commerce Bank* and *Sackett*.

LeBlanc v. Texas Commerce Bank

In *Texas Commerce Bank*, I represented the plaintiff, my neighbor Art Leblanc, a good Aggie and former member and president of the Spring Branch ISD Board of Trustees, another of my clients. Art and his father had been in business in Houston for about 50 years, and they were without a doubt one of the premier construction companies in Houston. They had regular customers such as Sears, Penney's, Kroger, and most of the major food chains. They also built many shopping centers for developers. Even during the worst of times, they remained profitable.

In the late 1980s, Lance McFaddin's nephew, Lance Gilliam, approached Art LeBlanc about building a theater as an anchor tenant in his proposed shopping center. Art, ever the cautious builder, said that he would be happy to do the work, but he could not start unless and until he had written assurance that the borrowing from the bank by Gilliam was in place. Time was of the essence. At this juncture the bank, through one of its officers, called Mr. LeBlanc and asked him to start to work immediately; otherwise, Gilliam could lose the anchor tenant.

The banker explained that it was absolutely necessary for Art LeBlanc to start to work immediately; that the loan had been approved orally; and that there would be a short delay in preparing the legal documents, because the lawyer was out of town. Art still refused to start the job. The next day the banker again called and insisted Mr. LeBlanc go to work, telling him it was imperative that he start immediately. So on the basis of this crisis, LeBlanc moved Heaven and Earth on this job and worked around the clock for several months, trying to make certain that the building was completed on time.

All during this period the bank assured Mr. LeBlanc that the loan was approved. Finally, after the expenditure of several hundred thousand dollars and the issuance of contracts and incurring of debts, Art had to pay his workmen and subcontractors, and he called the bank for money. It was at this time he received the word that the bank had decided *not* to fund the loan and had forgotten to tell Mr. LeBlanc. You get the picture.

We tried this case in front of Judge Hugo Touchy with a jury. Judge Touchy never saw a defendant he didn't like. He hated plaintiffs. We were no exception. He was hell-bent on not letting us win this lawsuit.

Before starting trial, my godson (called as such for lack of a better term) Mike Stevens, Hunt's lifetime friend, told me he had never seen a case tried, and that he wanted to come every day and observe in the courtroom. First of all, it's important that the readers of this epistle understand that Mike Stevens is not a lawyer and never was. But he was one of the best real estate developers in the world.

Mike did attend the trial every day, and he really went all out. He knew the case. He read the depositions. He met all of the witnesses. He gave me the benefit of his experience in trying to select the jury (he knew nothing), and then during the trial he busily wrote me questions to ask each of the witnesses. At one point, I had to make him sit down to keep this nonlawyer from making objections to some of the testimony in the courtroom! (Notwithstanding Mike's statements that he hates lawyers and lawsuits, he is the greatest case of a wannabe lawyer I have ever seen.) As I said, he went all out.

It was finally during my closing argument that Mike wrote furiously on his yellow pad, handing me page after page of handwritten notes, insisting that I use them in my closing argument. Judge Touchy wasn't sure who he was. Neither was I. The jury thought he was my law partner. My client had no idea who he was, and the client's wife thought Mike was Paul Newman, the movie actor. (I'm kidding about much of this, but it was a lot of fun.)

Finally, despite the judge's penchant for trying to keep the jury award to a minimum, justice prevailed and we won the case for Art LeBlanc.

My closing argument is worth noting, because it is now used throughout the courthouse from time to time, and I hear my argument, or of it, from many of the judges. I told the jury that if they looked at the top of the Harris County Civil Courts Building, they would see that there was no statue of Justice. There is a pedestal for that statue, but justice has never reigned over our courthouse. And I asked the jury to take it upon themselves to put Justice back at our courthouse. I told them that 20 years hence, as they were riding down the streets of Houston, they could point out to their children and grandchildren, "See that courthouse without the statue of Justice? Years, ago, in *LeBlanc v. Texas Commerce Bank*, I brought Justice back to the courthouse."

The jury gave us approximately $4 million. It was not enough. I handled the case on a contingent basis, and for quite some time

◄ TOUCHED BY GRACE

I was pestered with demand letters from "Attorney Stevens," demanding his share of the fee. (I would never tell him this, but he really would have made a great lawyer.)

Now we have a beautiful new civil courthouse in downtown Houston, also with no statue of justice anywhere in sight. That is still being done by Texas juries.

Harris County Child Protective Services v. Sackett

In all my experience at the courthouse, the very best came nearly last-or at what I thought would be the end of my career and on to retirement. Since that case, there have been other, similar cases around the country, but this was the first I knew about.

In February of 1991 my friend Bill Gothard called me and asked me if I would help a family who desperately needed a lawyer, and who had no money with which to pay. It seemed that Olga and Steve Sackett's middle daughter, Sarah, had non-Hodgkins lymphoma. She was desperately ill. The Sacketts' doctor, Dr. Boone, a well-known doctor and great Christian, had recommended that Sarah be placed in Texas Children's Hospital for treatment.

Things went badly. The Texas Children's doctor demanded that the Sacketts agree to immediate surgery and to immediate specialized treatment. The Sacketts asked for a moment to pray about it, but the doctor was still demanding immediate treatment. While asking the Lord for guidance, the doctor's associate rushed up to the doctor and in the presence of the Sacketts, told the doctor he had made a misdiagnosis; that Sarah's condition would require a different treatment; and that a bone graft needed to take place immediately. By this time the Sacketts had lost all trust in the doctor and decided to remove Sarah from the hospital and get a second opinion.

WINDING DOWN

Because the Sacketts had requested time for prayer, this egomaniac of a doctor jumped to the conclusion that the Sacketts were religious fanatics and irresponsible parents. He immediately filed an affidavit with the Children's Protective Service, requesting that the State of Texas, through the courts, terminate the parental rights of the Sacketts! Unbelievable. Take away the rights of the parents and let a state agency decide what was best for their child.

In the meantime, Olga Sackett had taken her daughter to a doctor in Indiana and also obtained a second opinion from the Mayo Clinic.

The irate and angry Texas doctor, discovering that the Sacketts had gone to Indiana, called that Indiana doctor and threatened to have his license removed because of his complicity in avoiding treatment that he prescribed. The intimidated Indiana doctor told the Sacketts that he was sorry, but he would have to take himself off the case.

In desperation, Olga Sackett took her ten-year-old daughter to the Contreras Clinic in Tijuana, "The Oasis of Hope." It was at this point that Steve Sackett, the father, called me and told me that he was due in court the following morning. Olga and Sarah were in Mexico.

Knowing nothing, I rushed to the courthouse, met Steve and his other beautiful daughter, and we proceeded to trial in Harris County Juvenile Court. The courtroom was full of the Sacketts' friends. My friends Skip and Anita Smith were there. People involved in Gothard's Basic Seminars were there. All of Houston was tuned in. At issue was the court's taking over Sarah's life and forcing her to be treated at Texas Children's Hospital against the advice and consent of the family. Fireworks occurred.

The judge was Judge Eric Andell. He was very experienced, and I knew of his fine reputation, but I had never seen him before.

The state started off the case with the Texas Children's doctor, the complainant. He testified belligerently that Sarah's death was imminent, that the Sacketts were irresponsible, and that they were, in effect, murdering their daughter! The *ad litem* attorney, a woman appointed by the Court to represent Sarah's interest, joined in the song that the Sacketts were killing their daughter.

Then began the testimony I will never forget.

The head child oncologist at M.D. Anderson got on the stand. He testified that he had examined all of the records of Texas Children's, that he was the greatest oncologist in all the world, and that he could state without equivocation that if Sarah were not treated by him personally within six weeks, she would die. There was no doubt in his mind about his testimony.

When it came my turn to cross-examine, I said, "Doctor, let's take a hypothetical." (I had just finished trying a case in Marshall, Texas.) "Assume that I live in Marshall, Texas, and that my ten-year-old daughter has lymphoma. And assume further there is no oncologist in Marshall, Texas. What would I do for my daughter?" This doctor, the greatest doctor in the world, then smugly stated, " You would bring her to me in Houston." I said, "Assume further that I have no money. What would I do?"

He said, "We'd take her free of charge, and you would bring her to me." I said, "How long would we be in Houston?" He said, "I don't know." I said, "where would we get the money for our travel expenses and living expenses in Houston?" He said, "You'd have to find it."

Finally he admitted that if I didn't have the money, I would have to take my daughter to our family doctor in Marshall for treatment. Then I inquired, "How would the family doctor treat her?" The doctor paused, a long pause, and slowly said he would treat her as if she had tuberculosis.

WINDING DOWN

I then asked, "what would be the percentage chance of recovery with treatment by the family doctor in Marshall, as compared to being treated by you at M.D. Anderson?" And the doctor begrudgingly said, "the same."

The state rested, and Judge Andell stood up out of his chair said, "Mr. Reynolds, call your medical witnesses."

I had none.

He said, "What about the doctor in Mexico?" I said, "Judge, there's no way to get that doctor here. I haven't even had the privilege of talking to him." Judge Andell said, "Let's get him on the phone."

And then I had an experience I had never seen in any courtroom. The judge hooked all the lawyers up to their own phone, had them on speakers, and Carol Wilson, who was helping my every move, dialed Dr. Contreras from the judge's chambers and hooked him up for all of us to listen.

Judge Andell asked Dr. Contreras, "Do you speak English?" Dr. Contreras said, "Yes." The judge said, "Do you understand an oath?" Dr. Contreras said, "yes." At that time, Judge Andell said, "raise your right hand and be sworn." He administered the oath, and Judge Andell said, "Mr. Reynolds, interrogate your witness."

Dr. Contreras was beautiful. He was a man in his 70s. He had been former surgeon general of Mexico. He had handled more than 49,000 cancer cases. His two sons practiced medicine in his hospital with him, and one was a graduate of the Oncology Schools of Mexico and London, the other a graduate of the Oncology School of Vienna.

Dr. Contreras explained his treatment, which consisted of small doses of some form of chemotherapy, but primarily megadoses of vitamins, together with another vitamin, (B-17), called Laetrile (which comes from apricot pits). He said that Sarah had been in his care now for a few days and she was already showing progress.

At this juncture, the judge stopped the proceeding and interrupted me and said, "Doctor, how long do you need Sarah to complete your treatment?" Dr. Contreras told him "two weeks." The judge then made his ruling, telling the father and telling me, and telling all the doctors and the public in Houston, that Sarah would remain with Dr. Contreras for the two weeks, after which she would return to Houston for examination and that she would be examined at M.D. Anderson Hospital by some doctor other than "the greatest doctor in the world."

The greatest doctor in the world stated that "it would be too late, and that in 60 days Sarah would be *dead.*"

We recessed. Sarah returned home in two weeks. She was examined at M.D. Anderson Hospital, and everyone met at the courthouse at the appointed hour. The courtroom was full. The TVs were blazing. Lawyers were everywhere.

Sarah was there with her mother and father and Carol Wilson was there with me. Skip and Anita Smith were there. Our little group stood together. And in came the new M.D. Anderson doctor, dressed in his green surgical outfit, with his green surgical hat, with an envelope in his hand. It was very dramatic. He did not speak to anyone, even his boss, the greatest doctor in the world. But he handed his envelope to Judge Andell as if Judge Andell were about to announce the winner of an Academy Award.

The judge opened the envelope, and without emotion, read the letter. Then without comment, he did not give the letter to me, he did not give the letter to the Sacketts, but he handed the letter to the greatest doctor in the world. The greatest doctor in the world than read silently the results of the examination. His first and only statement was, "There has been a mistake."

And the judge said, "Yes, Doctor, and you're it."

The report showed that Sarah Sackett was free of cancer. The judge then dismissed the case, and Sarah Sackett today is a beautiful young lady who is still free of cancer and is happily married to a minister of the gospel. They are raising two beautiful children in a Christian family. We hear from them every Christmas and sometimes at other times of the year. They became very important in our lives.

Can you think of a better way to end a law career?

My Law Partners

After reading the preceding stories about some of my lawsuits, you must realize that I had plenty of help in representing and winning for all these clients. Great lawyers make great law firms. For 21 years, Reynolds, Allen & Cook (which had a few other names) was the leading boutique litigation firm in Houston. I had great law partners, most of whom were-and still are-great trial lawyers.

Grant Cook especially is a terrific lawyer. He has a gift for it and a sense of humor that makes him outstanding. Jim Leahy, Stan Binion, Ed Junell, Mike Swan, Fred McClure, Charles Peterson, Tom Cordell, Kay Morgan, Charley Moore, Brent Baker, Bucky Cunningham, Don Looper, Cary Gray, Lamar McCorkle, Olan Boudreaux, Mike Swan, Jim Reed, Jim McGraw, and many others who I'll kick myself later for not remembering at this moment, were great and have gone on to make their fortunes and reputations without my help.

David Allen was very special, and he devoted his time to the corporate side of the firm. We were a Great Team. It was one of the saddest times of my life in the summer of 1980 when David Allen was killed in a car wreck on a mountain highway as his car was struck by a drunk driver on the wrong side of the road.

But as you read about these cases, it must be noted that I always had help, even though it seemed that I got all the glory. In my memoirs I may say "I won the case," but in most cases, it was really Bucky Cunningham, or Grant Cook, or Ed Junell, or Jim Leahy, or Mike Swan, or Stan Binion, or Cary Gray, or Tom Cordell, or John Tyler who was the real winner. The list is way too long, and I know how blessed I have been to have such talent working with me. There are too many cases where someone else did the lion's share of the work and I took the glory.

We had a great law firm, and great lawyers paved the way for me. After my heart valve problem, when the doctor told me I had to take it easy and could no longer head up a large firm, these talented lawyers went on to become even greater as they went to other firms and formed their own. I have been so proud of all of them.

But as my health improved, I longed to get back in the arena, so I formed a small firm with Bucky Cunningham, Charles Peterson, Tom Cordell, and Kay Morgan. We had some fun in those days of Reynolds, Cunningham, Peterson & Cordell. Then the doctors intervened once more and told me I had to wind it down in earnest. So after that, I became Of Counsel to Andrews & Kurth and then to Schwartz Junell Greenberg & Oathout, where my name is listed today.

But I have to repeat it just once more: none of the victories I've talked about could have been done without the help of all of my partners. I have truly had a charmed life as a lawyer. I have lived in Houston when Houston was the hub of the world. In these pages I have given only a smattering of the lifetime of lawsuits that I've tried. There are many others that should be mentioned. Likewise, if there were a way to do it, without omitting someone who needs to be recalled, I would prepare an Honor Roll of Lawyers, Partners, Associates, Secretaries, and Judges who have been a part of my life. Sufficeth to say, my family, who will be the main readers of this epistle, know all of these people by heart. They have stood with me and are truly responsible for the success that God has given me.

Sadly, many of these great lawyers and friends have passed on. As I write this, I've just had my 88th birthday, and I don't quite feel ready to quit. But my knees are bad, my heart is weak, diuretics make fluid build up around my lungs and heart, so it's difficult to walk for any distance, but Dr. Leachman is keeping me going, and I am grateful. Now it's really time to think seriously about retiring-or at least saying "No" every now and then.

Several years ago, I was speaking to the graduating class of Memorial High School, and in that speech I made a statement: "If I had a thousand lives to live, I'd be a lawyer in every one of them, right here in Houston, Texas."

Lately I've been giving that statement closer thought. Likewise, I have said on a number of occasions to my beautiful Susie that when I die, she has to promise me that the hearse that carries my body will make one pass around the courthouse. She said, "No way, José."

CHAPTER **16**

Legal Leftovers

In any trial lawyer's life, there are little anecdotal stories that flit around the brain and sometimes cause him or her to wake up in the night. Sometimes I wish I had written them down. Other times I tell the stories and then forget about them. Some are unforgettable, and since I'm told that readers will enjoy them, I have included several of these anecdotes in this chapter. It's good to have a place to put them.

꽃꽃꽃

Tom Alexander passed away on November 2, 2008. He was a great and famous Houston attorney, and stories about him abound. In one case I remember, Tom Alexander and David Seikel were on the other side, and they were then with Butler & Binion. In closing argument Alexander said I was one of his buddies and close friends, and he loved me, and that normally he liked to see me win, but in this case I was wrong and the jury needed to teach me-his old friend-a lesson. I got up and said, "You've seen me for three weeks and you've seen him for three weeks. Do you think I could be friends with the likes of him?" The jury roared.

It seems that I've tried more lawsuits with Tom Alexander on the other side than any other lawyer. As I said, Alexander was a great lawyer, but he had one fault, and that was, he always had too much work to do. And because of his volume of cases, there were occasions when I didn't think he was as prepared as he would have liked to have been. But don't let this fool you. What Alexander lacked in preparation, he made up with stand-up comedy. He was a born comedian who could kill you by making you laugh yourself to death. He was a worthy adversary.

And without going into individual cases Tom and I tried against each other over the years, I have to relate my favorite Alexander story. He was the most difficult man in America to talk to on the telephone. He did not return phone calls. And the reason probably was that he was never in his office. (This was before cell phones were permanent fixtures.)

Some years ago, I desperately needed to talk with him, and I finally got hold of the lady who worked for him, who ran his office, and she told me, "Mr. Reynolds, truthfully, Mr. Alexander's office is at the courthouse, and if you need to talk to Mr. Alexander, you need to talk to him at the courthouse."

About two weeks later, I was in Judge David West's court on a case totally unrelated to Alexander, and I was in the middle of presenting my very learned argument on a motion for summary judgment. Right in the middle of my argument, the phone at the judge's bench rang, and the judge said, "Excuse me, Mr. Reynolds." And with that, the judge picked up his phone and said into the phone, "Yes." Then he handed me the phone and said, "Mr. Alexander is returning your call."

꩜

Another favorite is the Judge Campbell story. I represented a guy named George Page. Colonel Bob Sonfield was the lawyer on the other side in the trial. It was a boundary dispute case involving a

LEGAL LEFTOVERS

survey problem. Red Washburn, the county surveyor, was my surveyor. He was asked if he did the survey personally, to which he answered, "no, my associate did it."

"Where is he now?"

"Korea."

Judge Campbell said, "Joe did you run into [Washburn's associate] while you were in Korea with General McArthur?"

※ ※ ※

I once was involved in a case where I had to take Barrie Damson's deposition. He was the Chairman of Damson Oil Corporation, which had namesake buildings in both Houston and New York. At this writing, I think he is now Chairman of Baseline Oil & Gas Corp.

Bill Wilde and Mark Lowes, from Bracewell & Patterson, represented Damson, and Charles Peterson and Tom Cordell were helping me in representing a German client. Tom Cordell tells the story this way: At end of the deposition, Mark came up and introduced himself to me and said he had heard a lot of great things about Joe Reynolds and wanted to meet him. (Remember, his firm had formerly been Bracewell, Reynolds & Patterson. Now it's Bracewell & Giuliani.)

Damson was infuriated that his lawyer would be nice to the opponent's lawyer! Damson said, "Well, I haven't heard any great things about him!"

Wilde stepped in and said, "Oh, Joe, that Barrie, he's one of a kind."

When Tom Cordell tells this story, he concludes it with, "Joe, without missing a beat, said, 'No, he's not. I sue his kind all the time.'"

Once I represented the famous heart surgeon, Dr. Michael DeBakey. It was a business case involving a guaranty on a note. While that case was pending, I got sick with hepatitis, and once again, Tom Cordell and Charles Peterson helped out and took over for me.

Tom Cordell tells this story as well: "While we were working on Dr. DeBakey's case, Joe and Dr. DeBakey were meeting one night in Joe's office.

"Joe got a telephone call from his granddaughter Jennifer called, crying, because she couldn't get to Houston for Joe's birthday. Dr. DeBakey said, "get her on the phone for me." Joe called her back and said, "Dr. DeBakey wants to talk to you." Dr. DeBakey got on the phone and said, "Jennifer, do you really want to come to your grandfather's birthday party Saturday?" She said, "Yes, I do." He said "Put your mother on the phone." Dr. DeBakey asked Jennifer's mother, Nancy, if it was all right if he sent his private plane to pick her up to bring her to Houston for Joe's birthday."

And he did. That's a pretty good act of friendship.

I once represented a landowner who had purchased some real estate that ended up being a toxic waste dump site, and suit had been filed by my predecessor firm in federal court against every petroleum and chemical company in the Golden Triangle area of the Southeast Texas Gulf Coast that had dumped its petroleum wastes on the land. The trial ended up in Marshall, Texas, and my friend Sam Hall was the judge. (This was that trial in Marshall, Texas, that I mentioned earlier.)

Again, Charles Peterson and Tom Cordell were with me in that trial. For one of the early hearings, there were about 50 lawyers on the other side, and I was sitting at the back of the courtroom, waiting for the hearing to begin. A lady came out and said "Is there a Joe Reynolds in the courtroom?" I got up and raised my hand, and she said, "please come with me," and took me back to the judge's chambers. Judge Hall and I had a long visit, while I'm sure the other attorneys must have wondered what in the world was going on.

The other attorney, Sim Lake, was invited into the Court's chambers, and Judge Hall, not having discussed this with me before, said to both of us: "Sim, Joe and I were in law school together, and we are very close personal friends, and our wives are close friends. So, unless you object, I am going to move the trial from Beaumont to Marshall, and during the trial Joe and his wife will stay with us, but I promise you we will not discuss the case." Sim Lake, normally a very quiet and reserved individual, turned purple. But I told the judge that, in view of all the help I would need from my paralegal and associate attorneys, I would not be able to stay in his home for that long trial. (With that, Sim Lake's color returned to normal.)

And a few years later Sim Lake went on to become one of the finest federal judges the Southern District of Texas has ever known.

This case ended up being one of the ones I lost, but it was based on the statute of limitations, and that part of the battle had already been lost by my predecessor, the firm that handled it before I got involved. I'll stop right there with that one.

Sufficeth to say that we thought we could overcome the problem. And if the jury had liked our client, perhaps we would have. But the jury did not like our client. And I must say that no matter how good you are nor how great your preparation, juries are judges of people, and it's not the lawyers who are on trial. The moral of this story is: *the juries judge the parties*. And it's a rare case where juries side with a party they don't like. So a word to young trial lawyers coming up: if your client is not likable, you need to find a way to make him or her likable.

Despite my loss of the case in Marshall, Judge Hall did not forget me. Several years later, he called to inform me that he had appointed me as a trial mediator to settle a very highly disputed antitrust suit involving a famous copy machine manufacturer. After a month of taking testimony and reviewing evidence, the case was settled, and my fee, which was decided by the lawyers and approved by Judge Hall, was a very nice sum.

Judge Hall has since passed on, but he left me with many, many good memories of a great friendship.

The Forney case was what is called a "bill of review case" that arose out of a divorce. A "bill of review" procedure is available when new information allegedly is discovered after the trial. My client was Mr. Red McCombs, who was the partner of the husband in the divorce case. Joe Jamail represented the wife and Percy Foreman, who had been the lawyer for the wife in the divorce case. The husband was represented by Jack O'Neill. In the bill of review, it was contended that Forney had hidden his assets in the name of my client, Red McCombs. This bill of review was to undo the alleged fraud against Mrs. Forney and her lawyer Foreman.

The bill of review case was tried before Judge Bert Tunks, with a jury selected to resolve the question of fraud.

I thought my fee was going to be a horse, as Red McCombs had asked me to come up to his ranch and bring my horse trailer. When I got there, I was presented with a prize longhorn steer, which I took to my ranch at Brenham, so Dan could take care of him.

My granddaughter Jennifer named the longhorn "TU," and I tell the fictitious story, especially to my Aggie friends, that every Thanksgiving we go to Brenham and beat the *&&^^%$# out of TU.

One day I went up to Brenham, and the longhorn was gone. Apparently Nancy had told Dan to get TU out of her yard and keep him from eating her flowers. So Dan took TU to the auction barn.

But the day wasn't lost. My neighbor across the road bought the longhorn steer at the auction barn and gave us permission to come to his ranch every Thanksgiving and "perform our ritual."

CHAPTER 17

Instant Aggies

My connection with Texas A&M was-and still is-such a big part of my life. That connection was brought about by my closest of all friends, Calvin Guest, who died in 2005. I miss him very much but know that Heaven welcomed him with open arms.

Calvin and I had been friends in the Marine Corps at the close of World War II. After that, we wound up together, along with Dolph Briscoe, working at the Texas capitol in 1949. Later, Calvin moved to Bryan-College Station and became the assistant controller at A&M. In the 50s he went into business for himself, and I became his lawyer and sometime partner in land ventures. Since World War II, we have been the best of friends. He is the key to my being an "Instant Aggie."

In the mid-'60s, universities all across America were in the throes of student rebellion and faculty unrest. A&M was the exception. General Earl Rudder, who was instrumental in the Normandy invasion and a genuine hero of WWII, was now President of Texas A&M, and as would be expected, he ran a tight ship with great control. But even he had problems.

Calvin got General Rudder to hire me as his outside lawyer. I handled some very interesting legal problems for General Rudder, which make for stories in themselves. After General Rudder's death, which I think was in 1969, I continued as outside lawyer for A&M, working for General Ludeke, the interim president. In 1971-72 this all changed. A&M hired a new president named Dr. Jack Williams, from Tennessee and other places. He was a smooth operator.

In late 1972, Dr. Williams and Dr. Mack Prescott, my friend and Calvin's best friend, were driving to Houston when Dr. Williams told Dr. Prescott that he was firing Joe Reynolds as Texas A&M outside lawyer and hiring Colonel Leon Jaworski. Dr. Prescott told Dr. Williams that Mr. Reynolds was a very good lawyer. Dr. Williams replied, "that may be true, but he has no political clout." On the way back to College Station, Dr. Prescott sulked and couldn't wait to call his friend Calvin Guest. Calvin was livid.

In November of 1972 my close friend Dolph Briscoe was elected governor of Texas, to be inaugurated in January of 1973. It just so happened that there was a two-year vacancy on the Board of Regents at Texas A&M that needed to be filled by Governor Smith, the outgoing governor.

Calvin got busy. He contacted his close friend Jim Lindsay, who was a close friend of Governor Preston Smith, and Jim Lindsay suggested to Governor Smith that he appoint me to fill this vacancy on the Board of Regents at A&M.

With support from Senator Moore and Senator Peyton McKnight from Tyler, Governor Smith called me in for a meeting, which was a good one.

I was appointed to serve as a Regent of Texas A&M University.

INSTANT AGGIES

By the middle of January, my friend Dolph Briscoe was Governor of Texas. My young law partner, Mark White, had been appointed Secretary of State of Texas, at Calvin's and my suggestion. (Mark White later became Governor of Texas.) Calvin was appointed Chairman of the Texas Democratic Party (there was no Republican Party in Texas at that time, to speak of). I had been and continued to be Governor Briscoe's personal lawyer. And now I was a new kid on the block at Texas A&M. I was the newest regent.

Dr. Williams didn't like it, maybe because he had just fired me as his lawyer. He resented me. At the first regents' meeting I attended, Clyde Wells, Chairman of the Board, and Dulie Bell, Chairman of the Academic Committee, took me under their wing and began to teach me the ins and outs of being a regent.

At that very first meeting I was told by my friends Clyde Freeman and Dr. Prescott that I was never to mention to Dr. Williams that they were friends of mine. Dulie Bell suggested that I become totally involved with academics because of my years with Houston ISD and Spring Branch ISD. Dulie suggested that I become the board expert on education. As it turned out, this was the reason Governor Smith had appointed me. I was to call the shots on academic matters. I took Dulie's advice and became the regent who dealt with the administration on academic affairs. My first board meeting was a dandy.

In the course of the meeting, Dr. Williams recommended that the regents approve a new Department of Rural Sociology. I had the gall to ask Dr. Williams what was Rural Sociology. Dr. Williams explained to me that everyone knew what rural sociology was. I pleaded ignorance and begged for an explanation.

Dr. Williams was irate. He had no idea what rural sociology was and in a show of temper commanded the Dean of Agriculture to explain it. He couldn't explain it, either. Acting as if I were bitterly opposed to the recommendation, Dr. Williams angrily withdrew the recommendation. I wasn't opposed to the recommendation; I just wanted to know what he meant by "Rural Sociology."

Things got worse. I casually asked, late in the meeting, how we evaluated faculty. In response to my question, Dr. Williams was insulting. He patiently explained to me, as if I were the most ignorant man in the world, that universities of the first class did not evaluate faculty; that was "high school stuff." Later, I would set up a method of faculty evaluation that became commonplace in universities and became the method of correcting the biggest problem in higher education, *i.e.*, the failure to get rid of incompetent teachers.

But everything came unglued when I made a motion at that first meeting that possession and use of alcoholic beverages on the A&M campus, with particular emphasis on the Board of Regents quarters, faculty activities, and the Memorial Student Center, be prohibited. Dr. Williams believed me to be the Original Redneck Southern Baptist. But by a 9 to 0 vote, the Board of Regents adopted the so-called "Reynolds Rule" prohibiting the possession and use of alcoholic beverages on A&M campuses. This rule remained in effect until one minute after I went off the Board, at which point the Reynolds Rule was put in the trash can.

Early on in my A&M service, Dr. Bob Cherry, Secretary to the Board of Regents, became my very good friend and advisor, and with the constant help of Clyde Wells and Dulie Bell, and armed with my new political clout, I became the unnamed leader at Texas A&M. This is the Gospel Truth. The Governor of Texas was my client. My best friend was the Chairman of the Democratic Party, my law partner Mark White was Secretary of State, and my cousin-in-law was Chief Justice of the Supreme Court of Texas.

Dr. Williams and I agreed to an uneasy peace, and Texas A&M grew and prospered. For 16 years my role was to be the education and academic regent. Others specialized in buildings, finance, sports, and athletics. But education and academics were mine. From the beginning, my philosophy was to make A&M greatest in the fields where it was already great, and not to promote future programs that would have no better than a mediocre future. This philosophy became that of A&M.

In 1974 Governor Briscoe appointed me for another six-year term. In 1982 Governor Mark White appointed me for another six-year term. I was off the board in 1981 and 1982, and I finished my last term as Regent on January 1, 1989. So I had the great and unique privilege of being appointed to the board by three different Texas governors.

Several years ago, Bob Cherry received a letter from Governor Smith telling Bob how proud he was of the growth and progress of A&M. In that letter he told Bob Cherry that after much thought, he was certain that his appointment of me to the Board of Regents was "the best appointment he ever made as governor." But I knew this was a great exaggeration and that he said it only because Bob Cherry was my close friend and had supported my appointment.

A&M became a great love of both Susie and me. I had the rare opportunity to see it grow from 16,000 students in 1973 to 41,000 students in 1988. After Dr. Williams, I worked with President Jarvis Miller, later President Dr. Frank Hubert, later Dr. Art Hansen, and still later Dr. Frank Vandiver. Each of these presidents had certain strengths. Each of them made a positive contribution.

Likewise, the Board of Regents had great members. Some I single out for special notice. Clyde Wells was a great chairman and a great man. Dulie Bell was a man of energy and commitment. For eight years I sat between Joe Richardson and Royce Wisenbaker, and the three of us became a team. They became my greatest friends. David Eller was a brilliant visionary. John Mobley and John Blocker brought common sense to the table.

But by far the greatest contributor was Dr. Cherry. To quote Susie, "He was the greatest." This was the strength of A&M. Together we preserved the traditions and the conservatism that had made A&M what it is. When I left A&M, it was indeed a university of the first class.

It is tempting to record many incidents, problems, or happenings. But I believe that this part of our story should be limited to my special involvement at A&M. One is the parking garages.

Automobiles are a major problem at the College Station campus. Parking garages were desperately needed, and (I like to think) because I fought the building of shiny, steel buildings on the campus, we still have a beautiful campus.

Once, while we were out in California visiting Hunt and Laura, they took us to dinner in downtown Pasadena and parked in the neatest garage I had ever seen. It looked like an office building and an atrium combined. I couldn't wait to suggest this type of structure at A&M. I did, and it went over big. As a result, A&M built two beautiful garages that didn't detract but actually added to the attractiveness of the College Station campus.

Also, I fought the good fight to save the greenery at the main campus in College Station by moving new buildings to the west campus. But by far my biggest contribution was in education. I promoted improvement in petroleum engineering, particularly in the fields of offshore platform and offshore drilling and offshore pipelines.

I stopped A&M from adopting courses in criminology, which was being taught very well at Sam Houston State University in Huntsville. I discouraged the development of an Art and Drama department, because Baylor and Texas had all that was needed. Likewise, I opposed a law school at A&M, because we needed another mediocre law school like we needed a hole in our heads.

I promoted and pushed Tarleton and Galveston to specific programs, and I insisted on the upgrading of the School of Veterinary Medicine and the School of Business. I took pride in the Department of Economics, with which I was involved. But by far my most strategic involvement was with the medical school. This is "the rest of the story."

One university in Texas had a brand-new medical school that could barely be accredited. There were many other medical schools in Texas, but only the Baylor Medical School at Houston and the Texas Medical School at Dallas were first class. The thought of a mediocre medical school at Texas A&M was of no interest to me.

Then one day I got a call from Dr. Jim Scofield, the Executive Secretary of the American Medical School Association in Washington, D.C. I had known Dr. Scofield before. He asked if I would come visit him about a medical school at A&M. I agreed with misgivings, but nonetheless, along with Dr. Prescott, I went to see Dr. Scofield in Washington.

When we arrived in Washington, we were also met by the President of the American Medical Association. The bottom line was that the American Medical Association and the American Medical School Association were asking us to establish a medical school. I repeated to him that we wanted no part of a mediocre medical school.

They explained that A&M, by their evaluation, had the greatest veterinary school in America. They stated that the pre-med and pre-vet curriculum were almost identical. They said that A&M had the best Chemistry Department in America, and for us not to have a medical school was crazy. They explained that Scott & White Hospital in Temple, as well as the VA Hospitals in Temple, Waco, and Marlin had agreed to be teaching hospitals, and that the head of the Veterans Administration wanted to see me before I left Washington.

They told us that the American Medical School Association had never asked any university to start a medical school, but they were asking us. I retorted that my concern was having a mediocrity or failure. Dr. Scofield responded that if we would limit our enrollment to 35 or 40 students a year, in ten years we could be co-equal to Baylor and Dallas. I said that I would discuss it with Governor Briscoe and let him know.

Before Dr. Prescott and I left Washington, we went over to see the head of the Veterans Administration, who just happened to be a great Aggie, former Congressman Tiger Teague. Tiger told me if we would build a med school, use the VA Hospitals as teaching hospitals, and emphasize in our med school the study of general practice, the Veterans Administration would give to A&M $20 million to build a medical school facility.

A few weeks later, after getting the wholehearted approval of Governor Briscoe, the Board of Regents voted to establish a med school at A&M. Four years later, while attending a board meeting at A&M, I was called to the phone by Dr. Scofield. He stated that he was calling us to congratulate us that it hadn't taken the ten years he had predicted, but at the end of four years, the medical school at A&M was co-equal to that of Baylor and Dallas.

The medical school, as all great schools and departments, warrants constant vigil. It is easy for a great school to slip into mediocrity and failure. But as of now, this medical school stands tall and is making a great contribution to our state and nation.

In 1987, during a meeting of the Board of Regents that I did not attend because of illness, I was called to the phone by Dr. John Coleman, who reported that the Board of Regents had just named the medical building for me. Again, I feel very humble whenever I pass by the beautiful Joe H. Reynolds Medical Building at that great university.

INSTANT AGGIES

Texas A&M has had some rugged problems because of ineffective leadership, but today as we write, it is back on track and is carrying the banner as one of the great universities of the world. It proudly stands for our Texas and American heritage and our great conservative traditions. That great school song at A&M includes these words: "When we've gone and seen the rest, we'll come and join the best; for we're the Aggies, the Aggies are we."

Someone said that line was written for this Baylor boy who became an Instant Aggie.

CHAPTER **18**

The Baptist and His Bible

If the preceding chapters of this chronicle were all there is to my life, I would consider myself a failure. I would have missed life as it is meant to be, and missed it abominably. Fortunately, there is at least one more chapter, and it is the most important.

The most important moment of my life occurred when I accepted the Lord Jesus Christ as my Savior, as a boy of 12. The defining moment of my life occurred at Iwo Jima, when I became a committed Christian. The crowning moment of my life occurred on a Monday night at Berachah Church, Houston, when Susie and I began a lifelong love affair with God's Holy Word, the Bible.

It's amazing how we got there. Both of us grew up as Christians. Susie fell in love with and married me because I was a Christian. Prayer got us through the tribulation of Korea. But it all came together that Monday night in the late 1950s at Berachah Church.

Dr. Kyle Yates had been our pastor at Second Baptist Church, where we all attended. Dr. Yates was a lovable, wonderful pastor, who was an outstanding authority on the Bible, and in particular, the Old Testament. And we loved Dr. Yates, but he never really challenged me to study The Word in depth. This was my fault, not his.

And then sometime in the mid-'50s, Dr. Yates retired. A pulpit committee was formed at Second Baptist, and Daddy Bo, Susie's Daddy, was Chairman of the Pulpit Committee. Dick Hammond, Ralph Ford, and I, all Young Turks, for some reason or another, were placed on that committee. There were other members, including Judge T.M. Kennerly, a local federal judge.

After many hours and days, our committee decided to recommend to Second Baptist Church that it call a new pastor. At the church congregational meeting, I was selected to bring the recommendation, after Daddy Bo had made the motion. I gave one of my greatest of all jury arguments, and the church enthusiastically called our new preacher.

The following Saturday, Dr. Ford, who lived across the street from Susie and me on Stamper Way, had an open house for all of the deacons and their wives to meet our new pastor. It started out as a great evening. But around 9 o'clock Dr. Ford, Dr. Hammond, Roland Heine, and I, and our wives, cornered our new pastor.

For some unexplainable reason I told him that I could not wait to hear him preach from the Book of Revelation. Susie and I had been studying the Book of Revelation at the church under the teaching of Mrs. William R. White, the wife of Dr. White, the President of Baylor from 1948 to 1961. She would come from Waco and teach us on Friday nights. We were learning and we loved it.

So at that fateful hour, I asked our pastor when would he begin teaching or preaching on the Book of Revelation? His answer shocked me. He told me that I did not understand the Book of Revelation; that not only did I not understand it, nobody understood it; that he didn't believe it should be in the New Testament; that it was full of symbolism; and since he was an A-Millennialist who didn't believe in the thousand-year reign of Christ on earth, he didn't teach the Book of Revelation.

This led me not to argue with him, but to carefully cross-examine him, trying to get a positive statement from him on the Book of Revelation. It was to no avail. He made it clear that he did not believe in the literal word of the Bible.

As soon as possible, Susie and I slipped away from the party and started across the street to our home, with broken hearts. As we reached the cul-de-sac, we sat down on the curb in front of our house, crushed. And I told her that next Sunday we would search for another church, where God's word was believed and taught.

It just so happened that I was coaching Hunt's Little League team at the time, and my assistant coach was the Reverend R. B. "Bob" Thieme, pastor at Berachah Church. We liked Bob Thieme as a person, and we knew he was a conservative preacher. In addition to his Sunday services, Bob taught Bible classes at his church on Tuesday through Friday nights.

That next Tuesday night, we attended his Bible class. Bob was teaching basic Bible doctrine, and I can truthfully say that Susie and I learned more that night about the Bible than we had learned in our entire lifetimes.

For the next 12 years, in addition to Sunday services, Susie and I attended Bible classes from 7 to 10, three nights a week. We learned the Bible. We were taught over this period of time the Book of Revelation from beginning to end, on at least three different occasions.

Likewise, we studied and learned the Book of John, the Book of Romans, the Book of Genesis, the Book of Daniel, and all of the books of the Bible. In addition, we learned in depth the various doctrines of the church, where they became meaningful to us. We could not learn enough. It was a grand and glorious time.

But all was not well at Berachah Church. From the beginning, Bob and I had this friendly disagreement over the meaning and application of one verse of Scripture, I John 1-9. This is a great verse in the Bible, and it was the cornerstone of Bob's teaching on the Christian way of life. I have no problem with I John 1-9, but I had trouble with Bob's definition of the words in the verse. The verse goes like this:

> *If you confess your sins, God is faithful and just to forgive your sins and to cleanse you from all unrighteousness.*

Bob taught that the word "confess" meant to enumerate your sins, without repenting or turning from those sins. And above all things, you did not need to feel sorry for your sins. I likened his teaching to Catholicism: "Confess on Sunday and raise hell all week." He told me that I was a legalist. I responded by telling him that he was an anti-nomanist. Sufficeth it to say, this difference was humongous!

We talked about it all the time. He, without mentioning my name, would make reference to this church member who was too hard-headed to understand the Word. I did not have his pulpit, and I did not discuss it with other people except my own family, but I didn't back down.

Finally one day, our mutual friend Sterling Hogan said, "I have a solution to the dilemma. Let's write a letter to Dr. Walvoord, President of Dallas Theological Seminary, and let him tell us who was right and who was wrong." It took a long time for us to get this letter written, but finally one day Bob and I agreed on it, and off it went to Dr. Walvoord.

Time went by. Weeks later, Sterling called and said, "Have lunch with me at the Ramada Club." I said "sure," and when I arrived at the Ramada Club, there were Bob and Sterling. We had a wonderful lunch. When we finished eating, Sterling said, "by the way, I heard from Dr. Walvoord."

He took out his letter and read Dr. Walvoord's comments. I still have that letter. I've kept it and I will treasure it all the rest of my life. But that letter didn't change Bob one iota.

You may think that this issue between Bob and me was small, but in truth, it was very big, because it had to do with lifestyles. And my concern was not for myself but for my children. I felt it extremely important that Hunt and Dan know the difference between right and wrong, and that they be taught that sin or a lifestyle of sin had consequences that could ruin a life.

So we said farewell and adieu to Berachah Church, being very thankful and grateful that we had had the great privilege of learning the Bible as if we had attended a seminary. We have never regretted being the recipients of a great Bible education, which equipped me to become a Sunday School teacher.

After searching, visiting, and attending a number of churches for short periods of time, in the early '80s we finally returned to Second Baptist Church, where by that time Dr. Ed Young had become the new pastor.

We immediately became a part of a modern miracle. Under Dr. Young, Second had grown from a church of one or two thousand members to more than thirty thousand in membership! From a church with a budget of $300,000 a year it had become a church with a budget of $25 million a year.

Second Baptist had become one of the fastest-growing churches in the world, and Dr. Young was an innovative, Bible-believing, Bible-teaching, evangelical, gifted Baptist preacher. He was dynamite. This church was dynamite. Dr. Young believed every word in the Bible. He was a gifted speaker. He was and is among the greatest preachers in America.

I had never seen anything like it. Every week, 50 to 100 people joined the church. Second led the nation in baptisms, and as I stated, Susie and I found ourselves in a modern miracle. He put us to work immediately. For some unknown reason, he designated me as his alter ego at the Southern Baptist Convention.

The SBC

In 1984 I knew very little about the Southern Baptist Convention. I knew Second Baptist Church was a member of the Southern Baptist Convention. I knew the Convention was an association of autonomous Baptist churches, who participated in giving to a cooperative program so as to select, train, and send missionaries around the world to plant Southern Baptist churches at home and around the world, and to train preachers at its seminaries to know the Bible.

I also knew in 1984 that the Southern Baptist Convention was the largest Protestant denomination of the world, consisting at that time of approximately 12 to 13 million members. Plus, I also knew at that very moment a great struggle was going on in this convention between the conservatives and liberals over the meaning of the Bible. There could be no compromise.

The liberal group were people like our former pastor. The conservative group were people like Dr. Young. The liberal side questioned the first ten chapters of the Book of Genesis, saying that it was legend; questioned other books of the Bible, including the miracles of Christ, and some the Deity of Christ; encouraged or recognized homosexual pastors; and apologized for the Biblical truth that Christ was the way, the truth, and the life, and that no man came to the Father but by Him. The conservatives believed

THE BAPTIST AND HIS BIBLE

every book of the Bible, including Genesis, and that the Bible was the inspired Word of God. The conservatives believed the miracles of Jesus Christ; that he was the mediator, and the only mediator, between God and man; and that homosexuality was a sin. And the liberals, who were in control of the convention until 1980, promoted abortion, whereas the conservatives opposed it and were strongly pro-life.

There were other differences, and some liberals or moderates might agree with some of the conservatives on some of the issues, but basically I have stated what the conservatives stand for. This difference between the two groups led to an epic struggle.

In 1978 the liberals totally dominated the SBC, but at that time God raised up a Christian judge, my friend Paul Pressler, whom I had incidentally gotten Governor Briscoe to appoint to the bench. Paul Pressler became a latter-day John the Baptist to lead the SBC out of the wilderness. By 1984 the conservatives had become a tenuous majority, and at this propitious moment my pastor, Dr. Young, said to me: "Go help Paul Pressler fight his battles."

Dr. Young was big in the convention movement. Second Baptist Church was the second or third largest church in the SBC. To carry the flag of Second in the SBC was heady stuff. Only the Lord could have equipped me for such a responsibility. The next 15 years of my life was not spent as a Marine, but were spent on the front lines of another war.

In 1986 I was appointed Assistant Parliamentarian of the convention. With Carol Wilson's help, I learned a little of *Robert's Rules of Order*, and she gave me a crash course, but I panicked at that first convention, where 45,000 messengers were voicing their positions and thoughts at one time. Believe it or not, order prevailed and so did truth. I served in that post for several years. I handled motions and resolutions during conventions and helped the messengers present their matters in a proper way. By 1987 the conservatives had carried the day. Truth had prevailed. The Bible was truly God's Word.

In addition, I have served as Chairman of the Nominating Committee, as a member of the Resolutions Committee, and then in 1990 became a member of the Executive Committee, finishing my final year in 2000.

During those years I was in the middle of things, including serving three years as a member of the 10-person restructuring committee that restructured the entire Southern Baptist Convention for the only time in its 150 years of existence. I had the great privilege of serving as an officer of the Executive Committee, and I had the great privilege of being one of the top ten laymen in the Southern Baptist Convention.

We laborers in the vineyard have brought the convention back to its roots of Biblical inerrancy. I feel a lot like the man in Ecclesiastes, chapter 9, which states:

> *There was a little city and few men within it. And there came a great king against it and besieged it; and built great bulwarks against it. Now there was found in it a poor, wise man and he by his wisdom delivered the city; yet no man remembered that same poor man.*

It was this little man, the common man, the man whose name is not remembered, who worked and stood for God's Word.

These words from the preachings and writings of Dr. Peter Marshall are fitting here: "This, the Lord's battle, was won by an unnumbered host of ordinary men and women, whose names are never printed; whose faces are never captured by the TV cameras; but whose quiet, unassuming labor makes the work of the leaders possible."
I was proud to have been a member of that army. Though I received

no medals for this service to the convention, I'm proud of the scars that came my way. From all those years of service, these scars are more precious to me than all the medals given me for my service in the wars of the Pacific and Korea.

Second Baptist Church

Meanwhile, back at Second Baptist Church, I found myself very involved. A church the size of Second needs a full-time lawyer, and together with Mark Schwartz, Kyle Sears, Kay Morgan, Carol Wilson, and others, this group of soldiers otherwise and erstwhile lawyers, had our hands full, spending hours and days on church legal business.

I also became a member of the Board of Trustees and eventually served as Chairman. The trustees are responsible for the church. It is here that I became involved with church staff, especially Lee Maxcy, and other great friends and laymen, trying to run an organization that is one of the largest churches in the world.

Truly, Second Baptist Church is a great mega-church. Its size and ministries are beyond one's imagination. On Easter Sunday of 2000, we had 23,000 in attendance. This staggers one's ability to understand what a mega-church is all about. If you have a question and wonder about all of this, my recommendation is that you come and see for yourself. You may not believe it, but you'll like it. Despite its size, it's the friendliest church in the world.

Nothing But the Truth

To use a phrase I've used before: The best is yet to come. In June of 1986, Dr. Young asked me to start a new Sunday School class, and stated that Mary Ann Belin, who was a member of the staff at the church, would be my co-teacher. This was great. Shortly after this, Mary Ann (who is Bruce's wife), Susie, Bruce, and I started the new class. As usual, my beloved friends and co-workers at the office, Carol Wilson and Kay Morgan, helped us get started. What a class! Out of deference to me, Mary Ann suggested that we name the class Nothing But the Truth, and that name became our message.

Mary Ann taught one Sunday and I would teach the next. This arrangement continued for about a year. Starting with the six of us named above, the class increased in number, the class increased to about 120 within a year. The class continued to grow. And sometime thereafter, the class was divided, and Mary Ann took half of the class and started a new Sunday School class. Evelyn Woodruff then became my co-teacher in NBTT.

Evelyn was a delight and a wonderful teacher, and the class continued to grow. Again, per the Baptist system, the class was divided a second time, and this time Jeanette Clift George and I began to teach together, but in order to make her feel a part of the class, we gave the class a new name, The Filling Station.

This continued for a couple of years, when the class was divided yet again, with Jeanette teaching a new class, and Dale Chapman became my co-teacher, until he moved to McAllen, at which time Gene Proctor took his place. After Jeanette left, the class voted to go back to its original name, Nothing But the Truth. Gene and I continued teaching, and Dale Chapman continued to help as we once again busily handled the tremendously rewarding duties of teaching this wonderful class.

But one Sunday morning as Gene Proctor, this great man of God, was teaching, he fainted and fell to the floor. A nurse in our class, Martha Fry, proceeded to render first aid. Finally the ambulance came. During the whole ordeal we prayed. Gene was rushed to the hospital. Soon after, Gene went to be with the Lord, and Gene became an inspiration to all of us.

THE BAPTIST AND HIS BIBLE

Our Associate Pastor Dr. Jim DeLoach became our co-teacher for a time. Not only is he a master teacher, a great theologian, and a supreme man of God, he is a great guy. It was my privilege to teach with this Christian Giant.

Today as I write this, Paul Pressler and I share most of the teaching duties, but old faithfuls such as John Tyler, Mark Schwartz, and HBU President Bob Sloane also lend a hand when we call on them.

I don't mean to imply that the teachers are the class; that is not true. This class is a fantastic group of people. We are a class of a hundred or more strong today, and it is composed of great Christians as well as great leaders in our church.

This class is the Rock of Gibraltar. Nothing But the Truth alone has established five missionary churches in Mexico, and one church in Brazil. We have planted and provided the seed money for these churches. In addition, under the leadership of Gray Wakefield, this class has helped establish Bible classes in churches in inner-city apartment projects. For example, Mike Stevens provided several rooms in one of his properties for our class to furnish an afternoon teacher to help the children with their homework, assist with sports programs, and to teach the Bible. On Sundays, that same teacher becomes a preacher and provides church for these children. Our class also provides leadership for the church.

The fun part of the class occurs right here at our home. For a period of about ten years or so, under the auspices of Bud and Gwen Insco, Nothing But the Truth held a May Day Picnic on what they call our "Front 40." This was a wonderful time where we all gather to sing, eat, and enjoy the fellowship.

Until the last few years, during the Christmas Season, our class built candy houses in our game room. I was usually kicked out of the room along about September of every year. Furniture was moved to the garage, and we built these candy houses as part of the Christmas project for the church, where they were all displayed. It was yet another great bonding time.

I was relegated to go get candy and under no condition would they allow me to touch the candy house project. For some reason that I do not understand, they think I am a cripple when it comes to doing things with my hands. One time after I had spent tedious hours putting graham crackers on the top of a Williamsburg house, John Mosely asked me to leave, and undid and redid all of my work! My feelings were hurt, and I am still pouting over their believing that I can't do things. (I say all this with a big smile, for it is, indeed, all true.)

This class is a family. There are many workers who keep it together, and I have to sing the praises of so many, that if I name them all, this book would be too long. And I surely would forget somebody and cause hurt feelings. So, as many others have done in this same situation, I will let it pass with that trite phrase, "You know who you are."

My contribution to the class is to teach. That's all I can do, and I love it very much. Susie, as usual, is the glue that holds all of us together. This class is brought together by that great chapter of the Bible, I Corinthians 13, and it personifies this class. "Now abideth, Faith, Hope, and Love, but the greatest of these is Love."

We have also established as our life message a powerful verse from Romans, Chapter 1, which states: "I am not ashamed of the Gospel of Christ. For it is the power of God unto Salvation to every one that believeth . . . ." As some of our members have died, any number of surviving spouses have told me that those words, "I am not ashamed of the Gospel of Christ," either have been or will be engraved on their tombstones. What a privilege it is for Susie and me to be a part of this great class. Along with my family and friends, this class is our richest asset. To God be the Glory.

But over the years that I have been writing and rewriting these memoirs, we have lost several of those valiant class members as God called them to Heaven. Others have taken their place. Today we are known as "The Gospel Truth" Class, and God's word is taught every Sunday.

Yours in the Fellowship of the Gospel,
Joe R.

P.S. In 2004 we in Harris County were battling the atheists who wanted a Bible removed from an encasement outside the Civil Courts building. I wrote this letter to Jack Sweeney, the publisher and president of the *Houston Chronicle*, and it appeared in print on Friday, September 3, 2004, covering a space about 19 inches high and 6 inches wide, with a big graphic of the Holy Bible and this Headline: "Heed Franklin's words in dispute over Bible's place." The next subtitle above my name was, "We forget God's role in human affairs at our peril," and I want to share the entire letter with you here.

> "I have followed with personal and professional interest the wrangling over the removal of a Bible in a monument on Harris County property.
>
> "The Aug. 26 *Chronicle* editorial, 'Bible study / County judge choosing to waste tax dollars on needless appeal that is both quixotic and wrong,' sent me to the history books.
>
> "As I read the theological and constitutional opinions, I was reminded of the greatest speech in American history.
>
> "During the Constitutional Convention of 1787, representatives from 12 states met in Philadelphia to draft a constitution so as to form a more perfect union. During those historic days, the delegates became extremely divided over the issue of what

authority would be given to the federal government and what would be reserved to the states. This divisiveness developed into anger and bitter feelings. It was at that point that the oldest and wisest delegate at the convention rose up and made one of the greatest speeches of all times.

"It appeared that all was lost, that there would be no constitution, and Mr. Franklin stated these words:

'In this situation of this assembly, groping as it were in the dark to find political truth, and scarce being able to distinguish it when it is presented to us, how is it, Sir, that we've not once called upon the Father of Lights to lead us in our deliberation? During the recent war with Great Britain we had daily prayer in this room, and our prayers, Sir, were heard and graciously answered.

'Have we forgotten our powerful friend, or do we imagine we no longer need His assistance? I have lived a long time, Sir, and the longer I live the more convincing proof I see in the truth that God governs the affairs of men. If a sparrow cannot fall to the ground without His notice, is it probable that an empire can rise without His aid? We have been taught by Holy Scripture, except the Lord build a house, they labor in vain that build it. And I firmly believe this. And I believe also, without His concurring aid, we shall succeed in this undertaking no better than the builders of Babel.'

"It was following this speech that these great men commenced starting their day together with prayer. And shortly thereafter, the constitution of 'We the People' was agreed upon.

"In a real sense I have spent my life at the Harris County Civil Courts Building, and I have passed and walked by that encased Bible more than a thousand times. It's very unnoticeable, and you have to be looking for it to see it. It can be easily avoided, and no one suggests that you read it.

"Several years ago I was trying a lawsuit in Marshall, Texas, and at the conclusion of our case I commenced my jury argument with these words: 'In the words of the Old Testament prophet Amos, I am not a preacher and I am not a preacher's son. But if I were a preacher, I would use as my text, 'Ladies and Gentlemen of the Jury, use your common sense.'

"The lawyer on the other side of that case was a young and outstanding lawyer by the name of Sim Lake. He won the case. But after my argument, Mr. Lake came to me and told me how much he enjoyed my argument. He told me that he liked the Old Testament Book of Amos and told me that he liked to make reference to a verse in the Book of Hosea. It's been a long time, but as I recall the verse, it was from Chapter 4, where God says to Hosea: 'Hear the words of the Lord. My people are destroyed for a lack of knowledge. Because thou has rejected knowledge, I have rejected thee. Because thou has forgotten me, I will forget thy children.'

"The Bible as exhibited at our courthouse could not be an embarrassment or offensive or a bother to anyone, and Judge Lake's opinion, as well as your editorial, shows a lack of common sense.

"One other word about the Constitutional Convention. As the convention was ending, Ben Franklin had one more word to say, and he approached General Washington, and our history books used to teach us that Mr. Franklin said, 'General, during these many weeks we have spent together here at Philadelphia, I have constantly noticed that chair in which you've been sitting. Immediately behind your head, carved in wood, is a sun. And lo, these many days I've been wondering if it were a rising or a setting sun.

"A recent poll by Channel 2 reported that 80 percent of the

citizens of this community wished the Bible to remain. Isn't it time for the *Houston Chronicle* and our federal courts to listen to 'We, the People' who, after all, are the authors of the constitution?"

My letter was published in its entirety in the *Houston Chronicle*, and I thank their editors for doing so.

But sadly, that Bible exhibit was later removed.

CHAPTER **19**

Health Matters

"You have cancer." Can there be any worse words to hear? Suddenly your life passes before your eyes and you think, "This can't be!" That happened to Susie in 1993. Susie, who had never been in the hospital except to give birth to Hunt and Dan, was being told she had the most disastrous health condition anyone could hear about.

I had been the one with the illnesses and maladies. From Iwo Jima shrapnel to heart problems that resulted in an aortal valve replacement, to complications from the frostbite I suffered in the Chosin Reservoir in Korea, to hepatitis contracted by eating shrimp in Amsterdam, to the years of chronic allergies, I was the sick one while Susie was healthy as a horse! Now, as a result of a voluntary procedure, Susie had been given a diagnosis, from a routine examination, of colon cancer. Fortunately, the operation got rid of all the cancer, without the usual colostomy such procedures frequently require. She was rid of that cancer, and all was well. But it was her first hospitalization for a serious illness, and it was a strange thing for me to become the nursemaid.

Years before, Susie had fallen for the usual mainstream medical prescription that most menopausal women are offered: estrogen therapy. She took estrogen for some time, and she is convinced that was what caused her next major medical matter, which occurred a mere nine months after the colon surgery: breast cancer! This couldn't be!

Let's let Susie tell the rest of this story.

Susie speaking:

> "I had a routine mammogram, and they said there was a condition that required a lumpectomy, which they did. The biopsy showed there were some cancer cells, and I was told I had to have a mastectomy before I left the hospital!" They didn't offer her the opportunity for a second opinion; they didn't say it might or might not require a total mastectomy or just another lumpectomy; they said the entire breast had to come off." Susie balked.
>
> "They told me I had carcinoma in situ, and I burst into tears." Joe said, "We'll go get a second opinion."
>
> "I did get a second opinion, and I had the second lumpectomy in less than two weeks." That doctor's verdict was the same: radical mastectomy. The entire breast had to come off.
>
> "During this time, my sweet friends Morna and Ken Wall and Skip and Anita Smith came to our house to have a special prayer meeting for guidance and direction as to what we should do. I also had the prayer and moral support of Jean and Max Crisp. I am living proof of the power of prayer, which is magnified when close friends pray together. We asked for guidance, and guidance came. I give the Lord the credit, and the honor and the glory, for any healing that I had, because He is the Great Physician, but I feel very firmly that he directed me to go to the Contreras Clinic and the treatment that made me whole.

"Four days after the second lumpectomy, Carol, Joe's wonderful secretary, Joe, and I , were on a plane to Southern California, where arrangements had been made for me to enter Contreras Oasis Hospital in Tijuana, Mexico.

"I spent the month of March 1994 in the Contreras Hospital, took their metabolic treatment, consisting of six grams of Laetrile intravenously per day, plus mega-doses of Vitamin C and other high-potency nutrients, plus a mostly vegetarian diet with fresh fruits, vegetables, and juices.

"The Contreras Hospital was a wonderful atmosphere of treating the whole patient, physically, spiritually, and mentally. There were devotional services, and spouses were encouraged to stay with the patients. We made great friends there. I was treated by both Dr. Ernesto Contreras Sr. and Dr. Ernesto Contreras Jr., affectionately called 'Dr. Senior' and 'Dr. Junior.'

"At the end of the month, Joe and I returned to Houston, where I continued to follow the diet and took Laetrile by mouth. In September of 1994, a Houston mammogram showed that the cancer was gone; my breast was clear of that unwanted invader! Whether it was the Laetrile or the thousands of prayers, or all of it together, it worked, and even today, ten years later as this is written, I still have that breast and both Joe's and my health is good."

Joe speaking:

Have you figured out by now that this was the same Dr. Contreras who treated Sarah Sackett and who testified by telephone in Judge Andell's court? Our Lord works in mysterious ways His wonders to perform.

TOUCHED BY GRACE

What happened during all of that ordeal was that I was moved from a position in support of mainstream medicine to a position in a quest for knowledge of alternative therapies. The more we searched, the more we learned about alternative therapy-about the power of vitamins, herbs, healthy diet, and healthy living. We learned that the key to good health is a good immune system.

We helped spread the word to many. Once Dr. Contreras Jr. came to Houston and Susie and I hosted two nights of programs where the doctor lectured on their alternative forms of treatment there in Tijuana.

"I met Don Factor, the son of Max Factor, who had come for a checkup, whose testimony was, shall we say, inspiring and enlightening," says Susie. "Five years before, he had been diagnosed with lung cancer, bone cancer, and liver cancer, and the doctors in London had given up on him, after they had radiated him and killed most of his good cells. I do not know how or why he went to Contreras, but as a result of it, five years later he was a very healthy human being."

There were hundreds of such stories Susie and I learned about in Tijuana, and as we increased our circle of friends in our search for information about alternative medicine.

We also learned that in far too many cases, the patients waited too late to come to Contreras. They waited until after American doctors had pounded their immune systems with rads and chemicals, and what little chance their immune system had to be strengthened by the Laetrile was long gone. Those were the saddest cases, because we now knew that there was a great deal of hope, if the patient's system still had enough good cells to work with to fight the cancer. What a shame that the FDA has banned Laetrile, which is really a vitamin, B-17, from the pits of things like apricots and peaches, as well as from other fruits, grasses, nuts, and plants.

HEALTH MATTERS

There's a great deal more to be said about this. For this was the greatest crisis of our lives, and Susie and I spent sleepless nights, worried about her future. We had taken a unique step. We had dared to go against all of the friendly, mainline medical advice coming from Methodist Hospital here in Houston. It was like taking a step out of a space ship. Everyone was telling us that we were pursuing a very dangerous course. But we felt good about it.

Not one time did we question the decision that we had made. We felt it was the Lord's will. And we believed that God answers prayer. We sincerely feel God heard our prayers. For all these years since those fateful diagnoses, Susie was been totally free of cancer. And she still is free of cancer as this book is finalized in 2009. To God be the glory. But it didn't come easily.

In the spring of 1999, Susie suffered a bad fall in the house and fractured her leg, which was treated by the insertion of a steel rod. It was a long recovery process.

Then in the spring of 2001, the cancer reappeared-the same cancer-on the same spot. It was found during a routine mammogram. Susie thinks it might be because she had become somewhat lax about taking her Laetrile. Another lumpectomy was performed, and the doctor assured us that he had gone well past the margins and there was no sign of its having spread.

We checked with the doctors and went back to Mexico for supplemental treatment. As I said, Susie remains free of cancer, and we continue to take many vitamins and herbal supplements to keep our systems healthy.

Susie spends much of her time advising and counseling people who are desperate for help and have heard of her story. Most of these strangers are persons who have been told by their oncologist that they can't be cured. The medical industry leaves these people with no hope. It is at this point that Susie tries to impart courage, hope, and love to fellow human beings who have been sent home to die by their doctors.

As we have walked in this valley, I have read and studied many authors on the subject of cancer treatment. I have learned for a fact that chemotherapy and radiation is not only not a cure, but that both of such treatments destroy the immune system and the treatments in fact become killers. It puzzles me that the billions of dollars that we have spent on cancer research have moved us backward rather than forward. The cure for cancer from these fields is most unlikely. Cancer is Big Business. When a cure is found, the pharmaceutical and medical industries of America will wake up one morning with broken hearts. Because for them, the well of money will have dried up.

There is hope. A few years ago, Susie and I were included in a very interesting get-together, where the leading oncologists of Houston met with some of the leading alternative practitioners in America, where both sides sincerely expressed the necessity, the desire, and the determination to work together to find the treatment and cure that is waiting to be discovered.

One famous oncologist has told me that future generations would look upon ours and tell us that these all-too-common megadoses of chemotherapy would be looked upon in the same light as the bloodletting practiced by medieval doctors.

We have also learned that diet is very significant in both the prevention and improvement of the immune system, which as of this time is the only hope a cancer patient has.

A few years ago, through the encouragement of our friends Archie and Geneel Crenshaw in Georgia, and Hans and Hilda

HEALTH MATTERS

von Lorentz in Switzerland, Susie and I were persuaded to go to Bavaria and be treated at Dr. Marten's clinic with live cell therapy from sheep embryos. This treatment has been commonplace in Europe for years, and it strengthens the body's immune system. We made two of those trips to Bavaria for the treatment. I was particularly improved, especially in my energy level. Dr. Marten has also explained that if I would exercise and reduce my weight, it would be even more beneficial.

Susie did not have the dramatic results that I had, but we had nothing to lose, and it's not harmful. Besides, Bavaria is the home of some of my dearest friends, and it is the most beautiful place in the world. So we always thought we would return for more treatment. We would love to go back, but traveling these days is just too difficult-especially airplane travel. Terrorism and getting too far from our doctors have pretty much ended our world travel.

Susie had another round of health problems in 2008 and that entire year was very bad. In trying to control her blood pressure, the doctors prescribed medications that gave her the most horrendous side effects. It was awful for her and awful for all of us. We went through a few doctors trying to get help for her.

Finally, we both got to the offices of Dr. Rick Leachman, and he has made the biggest difference in the world in both of us. He is a miracle worker. And he promised Michael Stevens as Michael was dying that he would "take care of Mama Sue." He even came up to me at Michael's funeral service and told me that story. We made an appointment to see him, and sure enough, we are now in the proper medical hands. Thanks, Michael.

My own health picture has not been without its scary moments. In 2000 I had a weird problem when a blood clot formed on a kidney, then wrapped itself around the kidney, and all but choked the life out of it. Through prayers, miracles, and good doctoring, despite the fear that they were going to lose me, I made it through that ordeal. And I will forever be grateful to Tom Cordell, who presented himself at the hospital and told the doctors to take a kidney from him if I needed it. Greater love . . . . But my son Hunt said Tom would have to get in line behind him.

As with most Americans, my health problems are mostly from my own doing. Exercise, even to a moderate degree, together with a moderate diet, would work wonders. However, even diet could not have helped my recent kidney problem or my aortal valve problem.

Like my mother, I was born with a slightly deformed heart, which fostered calcification of the aorta. It all came to a head one morning at 4 a.m., after weeks of a strenuous lawsuit, when I couldn't sleep. I got up and jogged in the yard. While jogging, I passed out, and lay on the grass for at least an hour. Unable to walk, I crawled to the house, awakened Susie, and she called Dr. DeBakey at home. He told her to get me in the car somehow and drive me straight to the emergency room, that he would be waiting. And she did just that.

At a speed that would make A. J. Foyt proud, she wheeled into the Methodist emergency parking place, and we were met by Dr. DeBakey himself, who wheeled me into the operating room. The rest is history. He inserted a plastic aorta valve, and after a long period of recovery, he changed his original opinion and relented, saying that I could "return to being a lawyer."

And, as I write this as 2009 comes to a close, I am experiencing fluid buildup in my lungs from time to time; the doctors have me on a diuretic that forces me to exercise, just going and going to what I now call the "Lasix Room"; my knees are bone on bone, and Dr. Leachman doesn't want me to have surgery.

And I am still trying to retire.

CHAPTER **20**

Conclusion

What more can I say? I've tried to limit my military experiences and especially the lawsuits that I have tried, to refrain from becoming a bore. I have deliberately left out many of the struggles and victories that were accomplished at A&M during my years on the Board. Enough is enough.

Also, I have fought the temptation to enumerate all my great friends who have contributed to my successes and stood by me at my failures. They are many, I'm proud to say, and I've mentioned some of those who happened to be at the forefront of my mind as I wrote. Someone has said that I miss the whole point of my life when I don't paint a self-portrait, interweaving the part that each of my friends has played. But to name them all would make a life story too long. No one knows better than I that without my family and friends, I would be absolutely nothing. Susie and I count our blessings and thank God every day for the wonderful people He has put in our path.

But I'm not really ready to conclude. I started working on these memoirs in 1995, and I've already lived longer than I thought I would. God has had more in store for me. And one of those things was something that has come to mean very much to me as I continue to try to retire. I'm talking abut my very special breakfasts with friends.

Several years ago a group of us Houston lawyers started meeting every Thursday morning for breakfast. We met at a place that is no longer there, but at the time it was Biba's One's a Meal on Memorial Drive, just a mile or two west of downtown and across the street from the very famous Otto's barbecue and hamburger restaurants.

When Biba's closed to make way for a center with several businesses, we moved our Thursday morning breakfast to Brennan's Restaurant on Smith Street, and the fine folks at Brennan's opened especially for us at 7 for these get-togethers.

These breakfasts came to mean so much to me, and it was as if I needed these gatherings to get my day off to a good start. Susie has never been a morning person, and frequently I would go out and have breakfast and be back home before she even got up.

I added Wednesday mornings with some of the men of my Sunday School Class, and we call ourselves "The PIGS," which stands for "Philosophical, Intellectual Gathering Society."

Then one of my favorite members of Second Baptist Church, Billy Branson, and I decided to meet every Friday morning for breakfast, and we have solved many of the world's problems over our Friday mornings together. Billy held a very special place in my life, until cancer took him to Heaven in early 2009. Now Bruce Belin, Max Crisp, and I try to meet on Fridays for breakfast.

Monday mornings were unfilled for some time, but I was able to schedule that morning with my prayer partners Jack Tompkins and David Nelson, and we try to get together when we are all in town and something doesn't prevent us from showing up.

CONCLUSION

But my life has been especially blessed by the addition of a group that meets on Tuesday mornings, and they include Dale Jefferson, Scott Link, and one whom I have grown very fond of and feel very fatherly toward named Wes Christian.

Wes and his wife Michelle have come to play an important part in the lives of Susie and me, and our lives have been even more enriched by their friendship. I met Wes through John O'Quinn, who has been a very close friend over the course of our legal careers. Wes was working with John on some groundbreaking stock fraud cases. I was immediately impressed with Wes, and learning that, in addition to being named Christian, he is a very fine Christian, he has become more endeared to me. I treasure his friendship and I treasure the good times we have had working together on some of his cases. I believe that he will continue to accomplish great things as his life and career wend their way through history.

Sadly, John O'Quinn was taken to Heaven on October 29, 2009, in a horrible car crash.

And the legal world has some fine "Young Turks" who have come up through the ranks and made me especially proud. I'll never remember all of them, but some I have already mentioned in these memoirs. Those who also come to mind are Wade Whilden, Steve Reck, David Finck, Gary Jewell, and Kelly Coghlan.

A special friend who means so much to Susie and me is Brent Baker, who has been so good to us in taking over the trustee and executor duties for us after Michael Stevens' untimely death.

So I am so thankful for all the special friends in my life. I know that God has put them all there for me at just the right times. There's no way I could do justice to what they have meant to me. I cannot even find a way to mention all their names, but I do thank them all and acknowledge each for the contributions made to my life. Whatever I have become, or whatever I have done, they have brought me there, and now I can truthfully say, I am what I am by the grace of God and with the help of my friends. The list of these friends is long, and with my failing memory, I would certainly overlook too many who are important. But you know who you are, and I will be eternally grateful.

And so I thought I was done with my legal career. I had "retired." Until one day I answered the phone, and it was Judge Lisa Millard, one of Harris County's finest family law judges. She said, "Help!" I said, "What's wrong?" She said, "My daddy told me when I was in trouble to call you. And I need help."

Her daddy was Judge Richard Millard, a buddy of mine from the Marines and later the judge of the 189th District Court of Harris County, Texas, who was then in his own state of retirement.

I dropped the novel I was reading and rushed to the courthouse. Judge Lisa Millard immediately ushered me in to her chambers and handed me the pleadings in a case styled *Carter v. Carter*. As I read the first paragraph, Judge Millard was telling me, "I'm appointing you as Receiver to handle this matter. The parties own a funeral home, and I'm turning it over to you to operate and handle this monstrosity." Linda Gayle Carter was suing *her wife* Connie Carter for divorce. Judge Millard said, "Handle it."

I got this appointment only a few minutes before the media broke the news. This was a first of its kind anywhere. Something was rotten in the state of Denmark.

I rushed out to the funeral home, which was across the street from the Veterans Cemetery, and I met a sweet lady, Connie Carter. I asked her how she could be involved in something like this. And with her eyes sparkling, she told me that Linda Gayle Carter, the plaintiff, was a hundred percent male! Connie told me she would help me run the funeral home pending the divorce.

CONCLUSION

The next six months was one of the most amazing periods of my life. I called a conference of the parties and their lawyers. I wanted to end all of this foolishness. And as I questioned the plaintiff Linda Gayle, he said that he could not take much of me, because I scared him, and that his doctor prohibited him from being under the stress that I was causing.

Rules and ethical considerations will not let me say anything else about this, but you can just use your imagination . . . .

I could tell you of the details of how I ran this funeral home for that next six months, all of which was an interesting experience. But the problem came to a conclusion when I discovered the corporate charter of the funeral home and saw that the applicant for the charter was Linda Gayle Carter, whose signature was notarized. I asked Linda Gayle if the signature of the notary was his [Linda Gayle's] former name, and he said "Yes."

The next day we met in court. The divorce was heard, and Connie was divorced from this man who was trying to avoid his creditors, and the judge awarded Connie one hundred percent of the funeral home. And Linda Gayle took back his true name and disappeared over the horizon.

So I settled back into my alleged retirement for a week or two, when I received yet another call for help. This time Judge Millard told me this new divorce case was a monster, and that the two parties together were represented by 18 different lawyers! I immediately called the lead lawyer, Steve Susman, who was not a divorce lawyer but rather a commercial litigation specialist. He referred me to retired Chief Justice of the Supreme Court of Texas Judge Tom Phillips, who told me that this case, in which he and Susman were involved, was "the biggest divorce case in history."

For the sake of privacy, I will not mention the style of the case, but this man and wife were fighting over $20 Billion. My job was to sell a home in California that was a duplicate of the Versailles Palace and a ranch with multiple stables, offices, and equipment, consisting of many acres that had been used for western movies.

The 18 lawyers gathered at my home, and my friend Jack Ogg was named as a mediator. He called for a mediation in California. At the time my friend and former law partner Cary Gray was involved in a legal controversy involving a ranch across the valley, and it just so happened that Cary was also a expert on horses and personally knew the foreman of the ranch I had to sell. When Cary advised some of his friends of the need to sell this ranch, it was immediately purchased at market price.

There are many other fascinating tales about this "biggest divorce in history," but it can all be summed up by this. When the case was over, the defendant husband knocked on my door at my home. After I invited him in, he said, "I just have a question I have to ask you. But before I ask this question, I need to comment that I think you were the best of all the 19 lawyers involved in the case. But what I don't understand is that you don't know how to charge fees for your time. All of the lawyers on both sides of this case became richer, and I feel like you need some help in charging fees."

I explained to this nice man that I was not his lawyer or her lawyer, but if he wanted to compare my fee, compare me to the judge. My fee compared to her judicial salary, because I was part of the court. The man said, "This doesn't sound very professional to me, but perhaps in my next divorce, you can be my lawyer."

Many other receiverships and court appointments came my way during my "retirement," most of which were interesting as well as amazing. But the last one was another monstrous estate, this time involving property in Colorado to be sold, and again one with

CONCLUSION

many lawyers and many hearings and never-ending discovery problems and gamesmanship by the lawyers. The case went to trial before a jury and millions of dollars later, it was finally settled and over with. Even the judge was chagrined to learn that the wife's lawyer, over the course of this long ordeal, had been paid a little in excess of $5 million. The property itself was bought by the wife at the appraised value, which was my sales price.

I started this whole story of my life with a statement somewhere made by me to the graduating class of Memorial High School that if I had a thousand lives to live, I'd be a lawyer in every one of them, in Houston, Texas. That still stands.

And as I close the book, I just received a call from the judge, asking me if I would be available to act as a receiver in another case. But my doctors have said I must say "no." They also "recommend" that I schedule only one thing each day, whether it's a lunch or a breakfast or a dinner, and even take some days off, period. I'll try to do that, and slow down a bit.

So this time I will really close this book with the statement that General Krulak said to me: "I'll see you on the beach."

As I reflect on these years with their many interesting people and stories, I realize the power of the statement that "No Man Is an Island."

And I know that I am so richly blessed to have been, truly,

Touched

by

Grace.

Epilogue

***

by Susie Reynolds

As I write this, my heart is filled with love and gratitude for the wonderful, kind, and loving man who was my husband for more than 61 years. What a blessing he was to so many.

Joe wrote the final pages of the preceding chapter on Friday, December 18, 2009. That night we attended our Sunday School class party, and when we returned, we watched an old movie, entitled *I'd Climb the Highest Mountain*, starring a Marine buddy of Joe's-William Lundigan-together with Susan Hayward. At the end of the movie, Joe kissed me goodnight and left to go to bed. Instead, right after midnight, he went to be with his Lord and Saviour, Jesus Christ.

When I was describing Joe's last moments to our pastor, Dr. Ed Young, he asked me, "What was the name of the movie you watched?"

I said, "I'd Climb the Highest Mountain."

Dr. Young replied, "There's the name of Joe's last sermon."
Joe climbed mountains his entire life. You know that from reading his stories. He was my mountain-climber, especially when I had health problems. He was a mountain-climber for his clients. He was a mountain-climber for Texas A&M. He was a mountain-climber for Goodness and for God.

I have been the most blessed woman on Earth. I miss him more than I can describe, and I know that so many others do as well.

I take comfort in knowing that we all live according to God's timetable, and that Joe will greet me when I get there.

God bless.

Appendix A
Mostly Complete List of Joe H. Reynolds' Reported Cases (chronological)

Thanks to Cary Gray for research and preparation.

A. **Appellate Opinions, Texas state courts**
   Air Routing International Corp. v. Britannia Airways, 150 S.W.3d 682
   McCall v. McCall, 24 S.W.3d 508
   Margraves v. State of Texas, 996 S.W.2d 290
   Maritime Overseas v. Ellis, 971 S.W.2d 402
   Granada Biosciences v. Barrett, 958 S.W.2d 215
   State Farm v. Simmons, 977 S.W.2d 541
   Maritime Overseas Corp. v. Ellis, 977 S.W.2d 536
   Matthews v. Home Insurance Co., 916 S.W.2d 666
   Hull & Company v. R. Chandler, 889 S.W.2d 513
   Canadian Helicopters Ltd. v. Hon. Wittig, 876 S.W.2d 304
   Bell Helicopter Textron Inc. v. Abbott, 863 S.W.2d 139
   Texas Commerce Bank Reagan v. Lebco Constructors, 865 S.W.2d 68
   Polland v. Lehmann, 832 S.W.2d 729
   Transamerican Natural Gas v. Hon. Powell, 811 S.W.2d 913
   Musick v. Reynolds, 798 S.W2d 626
   Brady v. 14th Court of Appeals, 795 S.W.2d 712
   Chase Manhattan Bank v. Hon. Lindsay, 787 S.W.2d 51
   Dunn v. Slagle, 783 S.W.2d 953
   Acker v. City of Huntsville, 787 S.W.2d 79
   Damon v. Cornett, 781 S.W.2d 597
   Archibald v. Act III Arabians, 768 S.W.2d 827
   Minns v. Minns, 762 S.W.2d 675
   Archibald v. Act III Arabians, 755 S.W.2d 84
   Archibald v. Act III Arabians, 741 S.W. 957
   Keck v. lst City Nat'l Bank of Houston, 731 S.W.2d 699
   Holmes v. Eckels, 731 S.W.2d 101
   Dodson v. Kung, 717 S.W. 385
   Smith v. White, 695 S.W.2d 295
   Humble Exploration Co. v. Browning, 690 S.W.2d 321
   Texas Public Building Authority v. Mattox, 686 S.W.2d 924
   Couch v. State of Texas, 688 S.W.2d 154

Driscoll v. Harris Co. Commissioners Ct., 688 S.W.2d 569
Humble Exploration Co. v. Browning, 677 S.W.2d 111
Shindler v. Harris, 673 S.W.2d 600
Robertson v. Gregory, 663 S.W.2d 4
Grimm v. Rizk, 640 S.W.2d 711
Redman Industries v. Couch, 613 S.W.2d 787
Cordell v. Cordell, 592 S.W.2d 848
Empire Life Ins. Co. v. Moody, 584 S.W.2d 855
Sears v. Continental Bank & Trust, 562 S.W.2d 843
Sears v. Continental Bank & Trust, 553 S.W.2d 394
McKenzie v. Farr, 541 S.W.2d 879
Nesmith v. Hester, 522 S.W.2d 605
Abercia v. First Nat'l Bank of San Antonio, 500 S.W.2d 573
Palm v. Lesher, 489 S.W.2d 351
State v. Sewell, 487 S.W.2d 716
Mann v. Perry, 486 S.W.2d 853
Farr v. McKinzie, 477 S.W.2d 672
Watson v. Sellers, 477 S.W.2d 678
McKellar v. Bracewell, 473 S.W.2d 542
Cummins v. Board of Trustees of Eanes ISD, 468 S.W.2d 913
Fourticq v. Fannin Bank, 461 S.W.2d 251
HISD v. City of Houston, 443 S.W.2d 49
McKellar v. Bracewell, 437 S.W.2d 319
City of Houston v. H.I.S.D., 436 S.W.2d 568
Pendleton v. Burkhalter, 432 S.W.2d 724
Harrell v. Harrell, 428 S.W.2d 370
Coffee v. Wm. Marsh Rice University, 408 S.W.2d 269
Swenson v. Swenson, 406 S.W.2d 245
Alvin I.S.D. v. Cooper, 404 S.W.2d 76
Southern States Life Insurance Co. v. Newlon, 398 S.W. 622
Martin v. Fannin Bank, 389 S.W.2d 724
Morris v. Porter, 393 S.W.2d 385
Coffee v. Wm. Marsh Rice University, 387 S.W.2d 132
Smith v. Southern Land Development Co., 385 S.W.2d 552
Houston Fire & Cas. Ins. Co. V. Riesel I.S.D., 375 S.W.2d 323

Nichols v. Aldine I.S.D., 356 S.W.2d 182
Davis No. 34318, 171 Tex.Crim. 629, 353 S.W.2d 29
Hand v. State of Texas, 348 S.W.2d 72
State of Texas v. Hand, 344 S.W.2d 467
Neal v. McElveen, 320 S.W.2d 36
Hart v. Ehlers, 319 S.W.2d 418
Noyl Corp. v. H.I.S.D., 317 S.W.2d 756
Estes v. Dow, 290 S.W.2d 561
Lehmann v. Krahl, 155 Tex. 270, 285 S.W.2d 179
City of Houston v. Schorr, 279 S.W.2d 957
Mayo Shell Corp. v. Lotz Towing Co., 279 S.W.2d 124
Krahl v. Lehmann, 277 S.W.2d 792
Richardson v. Lingo, 274 S.W.2d 883
Hegar v. Tucker, 274 S.W.2d 752
Richardson v. Lingo, 273 S.W.2d 119
Houston Shell & Concrete v. Minella, 269 S.W.2d 953
S. J. Kelley Const. Co. v. Page, 269 S.W.2d 689
Sinclair Houston Federal Credit Union v. Hendricks, 268 S.W.2d 290
Lloyds Cas. Insurer v. Shafer, 267 S.W.2d 588
Kennedy v. Holland, 267 S.W.2d 283
Stanley v. Columbus State Bank, 258 S.W.2d 840
State Board of Ins. v. Fulton, 149 Tex. 347, 234 S.W.2d 389
City of Houston v. Shilling, 235 S.W.2d 929
City of Houston v. Schorr, 231 S.W.2d 740
Texas State Hwy. Dept. v. Kinsler, 230 S.W.2d 364
State Board of Ins. Commissioners of Texas v. Fulton, 229 S.W.2d 652
Suburban Club, Inc. v. State, 222 S.W.2d 321

B. **Appellate Opinions, United States Courts of Appeals**
H.I.S.D. v. Ross, 364 U.S. 803, 81 S. Ct. 27
Shelton v. Exxon Corp., 843 F.2d 212
Union City Barge Line, Inc. v. Union Carbide Corp., 823 F.2d 129
Holloway v. Walker, 811 F.2d 263
Holloway v. Walker, 790 F.2d 1170
Holloway v. Walker, 784 F.2d 1287

Holloway v. Walker, 784 F.2d 1294
Holloway v. Walker, 765 F.2d 517
Crutcher v. Aetna Life Ins. Co., 746 F.2d 1076
Nissan Motor Corp. v. Harding, 739 F.2d 1005
Chemetron Corp. v. Business Funds, 718 F.2d 725
Meyers v. Moody, 693 F.2d 1196
United States v. Hajecate, 683 F.2d 894
Chemetron Corp. v. Business Funds, 682 F.2d 1149
United States v. Ballard v. Granlund, 663 F.2d 534
Darrow v. Southdown, Inc., 574 F.2d 1333
Schlesinger v. Wallace, 513 F.2d 65
Mendenhall v. Fleming Co., 504 F.2d 879
McCullough v. Lohn, 483 F.2d 34
United States v. Board of Trustees of Crosby I.S.D., 424 F.2d 625
Broussard v. H.I.S.D., 403 F.2d 34
Broussard v. H.I.S.D., 395 F.2d 817
Greater Houston Chap. American Civil Liberties Union v. H.I.S.D., 391 F.2d 599
Hightower v. McFarland, 355 F.2d 468
Texsteam Corp. v. Blanchard, 352 F.2d 983
David v. Phinney, 350 F.2d 371
Miller v. Barnes, 328 F.2d 810
Ross v. Dyer, 312 F.2d 191
Harrison v. Phillips, 289 F.2d 927
H.I.S.D. v. Ross, 282 F.2d 95

C. Opinions from United States District Courts

New Bremen Corp. v. Columbia Gas Transmission, 913 F. Supp. 985
F.D.I.C. v. Daniel, 158 F.R.D. 101
Massachusetts Mutual Life Ins. Co. v. Shoemaker, 849 F. Supp. 30
Shelton v. Exxon, 719 F. Supp. 537
Federal Savings & Loan Ins. Corp. v. First Nat'l Dev. Corp., 497 F. Supp. 724
In Re: Tenneco Securities Litigation, 449 F. Supp. 528
Gay v. Wheeler, 363 F. Supp. 764

Graham v. H.I.S.D., 335 F. Supp. 1164
Smith v. United States of America, 278 F. Supp. 230
Smith v. United States of America, 266 F. Supp. 824
Broussard v. H.I.S.D., 262 F. Supp. 266
Ross v. Dyer, 203 F. Supp. 124
Harrison v. Phillips, 185 F. Supp. 204135
Milner v. National Airlines, 23 F.R.D. 7

D. Tax Court

Watson v. Commissioner of Internal Revenue, T.C. Memo. 1977-268, 1977 WL 3559 (U.S. Tax Ct.)

The above list was compiled from reported cases that list Joe H. Reynolds as one of the attorneys. There are others in which Joe H. Reynolds tried the case but did not participate in the appeal or have his name on the briefs, and thus would not be found in a search.

Appendix B
Poems of Joe H. Reynolds

COLORADO TRAIL

*Sitting alone in Dillon Park
I wondered where we'd missed the mark,
And moralized upon the decay
Of the pioneer spirit in modern day.*

*Where are the men who once went forth
To battle giants and trust the Lord?*

*They came this way and discovered gold,
They built their homes and then grew old.*

*The sons of sons live here now,
But most of them have forgotten how
The West was won by these great men,
Who tried and failed, but tried again.*

*Today they seek a cozy nest,
And expect the government to do the rest.*

*The will to win is almost lost,
They want the Crown without the Cross.*

*So take me back to Dillon Park
And give, oh give me, a stronger heart
To raise my sons to walk and stand
And find, alas, the Promised Land.*

JOE H. REYNOLDS
September 1989
Houston, Texas

RETURN TO DILLON

Another time, another place,
I returned to Dillon's Park;
The trees were green,
The mountains high,
But something hurt my heart.

God's handiwork was just the same;
Great beauty was still there.
I asked a native what had changed,
And he said, "Progress is in the air.

People have found the Golden West;"
This time they came by plane;
Forgotten are the iron horse
And covered wagon fame.

The mining camps are long since gone;
The rush for gold is done;

But this time they didn't come for gold;
This time they came for fun.

Joe H. Reynolds
Circa 1994

KOREA 1950

One bitter night near Koto-Ri,
I captured one of the enemy.
He read my eyes and knew the deal-
He knew at once I had to kill.

In broken English, he made request
To see the picture in his vest.
I nodded "Yes" above battle noise,
And stared with him at wife and boys.

"Go!" I screamed. "Get out of here!"
He turned and ran and disappeared.
Oft I've wondered if he made it home-
Or is he buried in Korea's loam?

Did he ever again his family see?
But I've wondered most,
Were roles reversed,
How he would have treated me.

Joe H. Reynolds
November 1991
Houston, Texas

FRIENDSHIP-AND OTHER THINGS

I once had two friends-healthy, wealthy and wise;
Both tall and handsome-about the same size;
Both public servants-one more than the other;
I loved them both-I just called them "brother."

Both played tennis-terrible game-
Brings out the worst-they played 'bout the same.
I played them both, tho' I seldom won;
Lots of great fellowship-really great fun.

They were just kids-least seemed so to me.
Look at 'em now-sad sacks to see.
But there's hope for 'em yet-you can just bet!

There's a gilded, golden gleam in their eyes.
They'll cut Old Man Failure right down to size.
My friends Hank and Joe-My friends Joe and Hank-
Names to remember-only the Titanic sank.

They're going to float-they may even swim-
And beat all these aches-get back their vim.
We've all been praying-loud, long, and hard.
Now it's up to you guys to get out in the yard.

Creak if you must-groan a bit, too.
Courage like yours belongs to a few.
The worst is now over-the new word is Go!
The world needs you both-and so-

"You only live once!" If you work it just right-
Once is enough; I think you just might.

P.S. The Lord loves you both-and so do I.
That just slipped out-goodbye!

Joe H. Reynolds
1989

A TRIBUTE TO "BIG JOE" RICHARDSON

A man so big in every way
We have the privilege to honor today.
His love for A&M we all know
But there's much, much more to our "Big Joe."

He followed his father in drilling for oil
And found many gushers through work and toil.
If you pricked the finger of this big dude
You wouldn't find blood, but maroon and white crude.

Today he drills in Belize, far away
A monumental vein, the geologists say;
Exploring that land is pioneering at its best;
He took the equipment, tools-and all the rest.

A serious accident at age 29
Nearly took his life, his sparkle, his shine;
A blowout plunged his car to a ravine
And he lay there injured, no help to be seen.

Two men came along, he was saved at last!
But these two crooks had a shady past;
They robbed Big Joe of all he had
And left him there, all but dead.

Joe's faith held fast, and help finally came;
But the end result was that he might be lame.
Down, but not out, he developed a shoe
It works for Big Joe-and for others, too.

His heart, you see, is even bigger than he.
He reminds us all of a big oak tree.
Respect comes his way from across the land,
For many know the works of this big man.

His giving to others has never stopped;
He relentlessly works to keep Aggies on top.
And in this building future oil men will grow;
Reflecting this man-Big, Big Joe.

Joe H. Reynolds
May 24, 1990

Poem Written by Joe Reynolds on the occasion of the birth of his niece, Carol Ann Reynolds [now Keele]

To Johnnie & Viola:

Seven days before Christmas
And all through the house,
Not a creature was stirring
Not even a mouse.
Now maybe you don't quite understand,
But this was the birth of little Carol Ann.

Her hair was quite black, two eyes of blue
And like her mama and papa, I'm proud of her, too.
She's worth more than gold
As time will sure tell,
Because if you offered a million we still wouldn't sell.
For I'm one of her uncles so please let me know
If you ever need help call on your Uncle Joe.

- Carol Ann Reynolds [now Keele] was born in 1938 and has this poem safely tucked away in her lock box. She has given her permission to reprint it here. Apparently Joe wrote this poem and sent it to his brother Johnnie and his wife Viola right after Carol was born, so he would have been 16 years old at the time.

Poem written by Hunt Reynolds and presented to Joe Reynolds on Father's day, 1990

On the plains of hesitation,
I have never taken a step,
Except for one of silence
I truly now regret.

Strong and independent men
Sometimes go their separate ways
I thank God for my children
Who melted that all away.

You have always shown
What I have learned in time;
There is nothing more important
Than the children I call mine.

So I can now express the long overdue
Because it's Father's Day and so true.
It was in the beginning as it is until the end
I love you, Dad, my best friend.

Father's Day
June 17, 1990
- HSR -

Appendix C
Military Timeline of Joe H. Reynolds

Sept. 1941: Joe Hunter Reynolds entered Baylor Law School

Dec. 1941: Pearl Harbor

Joe had just turned 20 and thought about enlisting, because he wanted to help with the war effort. But both Dean Jackson and Judge Hale of the Waco Court of Appeals said "No." So he doubled up and attended through summer.

Fall 1942: A young Marine came to the school and was the Chapel speaker, on crutches, in his dress blues, and looking like a movie star. He told of his experience at Guadalcanal and said, "If any of you young men want to kill Japs, meet me outside."

Joe was first in line. He joined the Marine Corps but was told to stay in law school until called to active duty. He went to Dallas, where he passed his physical. By doubling up at Baylor Law, he finished his second year of law school.

July 1, 1943: Joe was told to report to SW University in Georgetown TX for further education before reporting to boot camp. He was there four months in the "V-12 Program" and took courses in Physics, Celestial Navigation, Calculus, Mechanical Drawing, and Obstacle Course Running.

Late Oct. 1943: Joe and others were selected for a train ride to boot camp and he ended up at Parris Island, SC, on an extremely hot day. Joe learned why some called the place "The Land that God Forgot."

After boot camp, Joe was named Number 1 and with 12 others was sent to Quantico for Officers Training. After six months of learning combat at Quantico, VA, Joe was promoted to second lieutenant and assigned to artillery school at Quantico, to prepare him to become a forward observer. He learned how to direct the artillery fire of 75-pack Howitzers, 105 Howitzers, and 155 Howitzers (commonly called cannons).

1944: Following graduation from artillery school, Joe was ordered to join the Third Marine Division, Twelfth Marines (the artillery regiment), in the South Pacific. The Third Marine Division made an amphibious landing on the Island of Guam in the Central Pacific, where Joe first met the Japanese in person, as a green forward observer.

The Marines easily wiped out the Japanese and returned the island of Guam to the good old USA, and Guam became the headquarters of Admiral Nimitz and the U.S. Pacific Fleet, as well as the base camp of the Third Marine Division.

Feb. 1945: Third Marine Division went aboard ship, destination Iwo Jima, landing 2/19. After several days of supporting the Fourth and Fifth Marines, the Third Marines were told to "Attack and Take" the second airstrip in the center of the island.

It had been on the first airstrip, either the first or second day they were ashore, that Joe looked up to the top of Suribachi and saw a very small American flag flying at the top. It was clearly recognizable. Sometime later that same day, a larger flag replaced the small one, and the Stars and Stripes proudly waved as an inspiration to all of the Marines on Iwo Jima and to the American people forever. But Joe didn't have time to keep his eyes on the flag very long, and he didn't have any idea that it would become one of the most recognizable art subjects in the world.

Seeing that flag atop Suribachi stirred his emotions to the core, and tears came to his eyes. That flag represented America and was what he was fighting for-something that was worthwhile. Joe says, "it may be corny, but to the day I die, I will see within my heart the American flag waving atop Mount Suribachi."

As they dug in on Airstrip Number Two, their ammunition dump was blown to smithereens. Joe thought the island of Iwo was going to break apart. Joe says that "If you dug one foot below the surface into the volcanic sand that covered this island, it was hot with heat from the volcano that was Suribachi. As a matter of fact, in order to even lie down on the ground, you had to put a poncho under you to keep your body from blistering."

Then torrential rains came, with Japanese bombs exploding everywhere. Joe spied an old airplane wing and pulled it over their foxhole while his buddy kept on lookout. A Japanese mortar hit the wing and hundreds of aluminum splinters pierced Joe's legs. He continued fighting as they kept attacking the Japanese in their caves.

They took Iwo Jima in what has been described as one of the bloodiest battles of Marine Corps history, and that little island became one of our greatest assets in prosecuting the War in the Pacific, as it became a haven for crippled planes returning from bombing runs over Japan. But Joe had developed blood poisoning from the metal shards and later he was evacuated to a hospital, where he stayed for many months.

Sometime while Joe was recuperating in the hospital from his leg injuries, he was awarded the Purple Heart.

Aug. 12, 1950: Joe was having a successful law career when he opened an official-looking letter that said, "Greetings-you have been called back into active duty in the United States Marine Corps. Ten days from this date you will report for active duty at Camp Pendleton, Oceanside, California."

Sept. 15, 1950: Three weeks from the day he left Houston, he stormed ashore at the Battle of Inchon, Korea, a First Lieutenant in the United States Marine Corps, First Marine Division, alongside Col. Chesty Puller.

Sept.-Oct. 1950: They had to fight the North Koreans for every inch of ground to reach Seoul, which meant attacking and capturing the Kimpo air strip. They finally encircled the city before its capture, and Joe was one of the first Marines to cross the Han River in the attack on and defeat of Seoul-a city larger than Houston.

The 1st Marines, of which Joe was a part, eventually reached the 38th parallel. On the way, they had many casualties and took many North Korean prisoners. Joe describes it as "a relatively easy campaign compared to Iwo Jima," but he was glad to reach the 38th parallel and thought the war was over.

Oct. 19, 1950: Chinese in massive numbers began crossing the Yalu River. Joe's 1st Marines were transported back to Inchon in trucks, then loaded aboard old Japanese LSTs and sailed north around the South Korean horn through the minefields of the Japanese Sea.

Oct. 26, 1950: They then made an amphibious landing in the North Korean port of Wonsan. Their objective was to reach the Yalu River, the boundary between North Korea and the Manchurian border of China, and they were told that on the way they were to capture the power plant at the south end of the Chosin Reservoir (the name was Changjin on Korea maps and Chosen on Japanese maps. The Marines had Japanese maps and thus called it "Chosin"). Their approach march was up a narrow valley, surrounded by high, snow-covered mountains, and their objective, the Yalu River, was about 100 miles away. So they marched north, through Hamhung, Sudong, Koto-Ri, and Hagaru-ri. Joe's unit was the artillery outfit for the 7th Matrines, and he was in Major. Fox Parry's 3rd Battalion, 11th Marines, and covered the advance of the 7th Marines to Sudong.

Nov. 11, 1950: As Joe was still wearing his light clothing, a norther blew in, and the next morning it was 11 degrees Fahrenheit. And it got colder; within two weeks, the temperature was 40 below zero. They were issued parkas, gloves, and shoe packs, and had to sleep on the ground. When asked how cold it was, Joe says, "It was so cold, our rations would freeze on our lips before we could eat them. The weapons we had were almost useless. You couldn't fire the BAR. You could throw your carbine away. The only gun we carried that could be fired in that cold was the good old M-1."

In a 1952 article in the old, now-defunct Houston Press, Joe commented, "It was so cold that your breath froze and the cold brought tears to your eyes and the tears became ice before you could dry your eyes. It was so cold that when we'd take a prisoner and pull his gun out of his hands, his hands and arms would come off in ours."

Thanksgiving 1950: With our soldiers having little to be thankful for, around midnight the Chinese Communists crossed the Yalu River into North Korea and entered the Korean War, and about 12,000 Marines were hit by about 100,000 Chinese soldiers, at Joe's position. By noon they learned that they were totally surrounded, and they were in the fight of their lives.

Nov. 26, 1950: The campaign began at Yudam-ni as the Chinese Communists attacked the 5th and 7th Marine Regiments on the west side of the reservoir. By November 28, the battle spread throughout the 1st Marine Division section of the area.

It was about this time that their commanding officer, Major General Oliver P. Smith, issued his famous statement: "Retreat, hell. We'll just fight in another direction." They formed a perimeter and fought the Chinese from every direction, moving as a rubber band, always moving to the south. They would stretch and pull up, and stretch and pull up, and did so for three weeks, fighting their way through the Chinese encirclement.

Somewhere along the push south, Joe was wounded in both feet by a Chinese mortar shell. Because of the cold, he felt no pain. But for more than a hundred miles, he walked on seriously injured feet. By the time they reached safety at Hung Nam, both of his feet were the size of footballs.

Joe was evacuated to a U.S. Army hospital in Fuka Yoka, Japan, along with many others. The first thing they did was to cut off his clothes, which he had been wearing continually for months. He was then thrown into a hot shower, where he came alive again after those many weeks of freezing. Several days later, he was transferred to the naval hospital and port at Yakuska, Japan. Of the 15,000 Marines at the Chosin, 6,000 of them were in that hospital. Joe spent a year recovering.

Sometime during the fighting in Korea, Joe was promoted to the rank of Captain.

And at another time, First Lieutenant Joe H. Reynolds, United States Marine Corps Reserves, received a Commendation Ribbon with Combat "V" from Commanding General G. C. Thomas: "For excellent service in the line of his profession while serving with a Marine artillery battalion during operations in KOREA from 2 November to 10 December 1950. First Lieutenant REYNOLDS, serving as an assistant operations officer in an artillery battalion, displayed great skill, courage, and confidence in the performance of his duties. Throughout this period he worked long tedious hours under adverse weather conditions, supervising and directing the efficient operations of an artillery fire direction team. During the movement of the division from Yudam-ni, Korea, to Chinhung-ni, Korea, he constantly exposed himself to accurate enemy small arms, mortar, and machine gun fire in order to direct the fire of his battalion on numerous enemy emplacements and road blocks along the way. His timely actions and complete disregard for his own personal safety were directly instrumental in the successful movement of the division, thereby setting an example for all who served with him and materially contributing to the success achieved by his battalion. First Lieutenant REYNOLDS' conduct throughout was in keeping with the highest traditions of the United States Naval Service."

Dec. 27, 1950: General Smith's log reflects his division's losses since the Inchon landing 15 September:

Killed in action:	969
Died of wounds:	163
Missing in action:	199
Wounded in action:	5,517
Total:	6,848
Non-battle casualties:	8,900
POWs taken:	7,916